Advance Praise for *SAFE*

"*Safe* is a masterful integration of neuroscience, attachment theory, and real-world healing. Jessica Baum bridges clinical insight with deep compassion, offering readers a road map for transforming the way they relate to themselves and others."

—JULIE MENANNO, AUTHOR OF *SECURE LOVE*

"Reading *Safe* felt like sitting down with a wise, compassionate friend who understands the ache of disconnection and the beauty of repair. Jessica Baum has written a road map for anyone yearning to feel secure, seen, and safe in their relationships."

—MARK GROVES, HUMAN CONNECTION SPECIALIST AND COAUTHOR OF *LIBERATED LOVE*

"A thorough and readable presentation that locates the context of wounding and healing in the 'space-between' . . . We strongly recommend this WONDERFUL book to therapists and everyone who wants a clear analysis of the relational dynamics of the healing journey and a clear path to achieving it."

—HARVILLE HENDRIX, PhD, AND HELEN LAKELLY HUNT, PhD, COAUTHORS OF *GETTING THE LOVE YOU WANT* AND *DOING IMAGO RELATIONSHIP THERAPY IN THE SPACE BETWEEN*

"Jessica Baum blends attachment science with deep compassion to create a practical guide for nervous system healing. *Safe* is a must-read for anyone who struggles to feel secure in relationships or is overwhelmed by their own emotions. It offers both insight and relief, using tools grounded in polyvagal theory and neurobiology. *Safe* provides real strategies—not just theory."

—TERRI COLE, PSYCHOTHERAPIST, AUTHOR OF *BOUNDARY BOSS* AND *TOO MUCH*, AND HOST OF *THE TERRI COLE SHOW*

"Relationships challenge us to our core, and yet they are the foundation of our humanity. *Safe* breathes love and understanding as we meet ourselves and our limitations with curiosity and compassion, and ultimately move toward becoming secure."

—SHELEANA AIYANA, FOUNDER OF RISING WOMAN

"What makes *Safe* so powerful is its gentle depth. Jessica Baum invites us to hold our protective patterns with reverence while guiding us toward true connection. This is attachment work for people ready to reclaim their story—and their worth."

—DR. INGRID CLAYTON, AUTHOR OF *FAWNING*

"As a couples therapist, *Safe* is the book I want to give my clients who struggle to feel secure in their relationships again and again. Jessica Baum makes complex attachment patterns feel not only understandable but changeable."

—ELIZABETH EARNSHAW, LMFT, AUTHOR OF *'TIL STRESS DO US PART*
AND *I WANT THIS TO WORK*

SAFE

SAFE

An Attachment-Informed Guide to
Building More Secure Relationships

Coming Home to Yourself and Others

JESSICA BAUM, LMHC

Tarcher
an imprint of Penguin Random House
New York

Tarcher

an imprint of Penguin Random House LLC
1745 Broadway, New York, NY 10019
penguinrandomhouse.com

Most Tarcher books are available at special quantity discounts for bulk purchase for
sales promotions, premiums, fund-raising, and educational needs. Special books or
book excerpts also can be created to fit specific needs. For details, write:
SpecialMarkets@penguinrandomhouse.com.

Library of Congress Cataloging-in-Publication Data has been applied for.

ISBN: 9780593850817
Ebook ISBN: 9780593850831

Printed in the United States of America
1st Printing

The authorized representative in the EU for product safety and compliance is
Penguin Random House Ireland, Morrison Chambers, 32 Nassau Street,
Dublin D02 YH68, Ireland, https://eu-contact.penguin.ie.

To my mentor, Bonnie Badenoch.

Since you have come into my life, you have deeply impacted me, my own personal healing, and the books I have out in the world. It is your compassion that has had the biggest influence on me.

I am in great gratitude that you have helped shape this book with your wisdom from the many years of studying interpersonal neurobiology, and that your compassionate tone is felt throughout these pages. So many of your profound messages are woven throughout this manuscript. I could not have created this without you, and I feel grateful that you have guided me in such profound ways.

From my heart to yours—I can't thank you enough.

CONTENTS

SAFE

INTRODUCTION

From the time we are very small we are taught the importance of being strong and independent. As linked as these two words can be in our minds, the truth is that we all need to feel that we are held safely in the arms, hearts, and minds of the important people in our lives. It is through these connections that we feel secure and protected in this challenging world. "Safe" is such a powerful word, reaching way down inside our bodies. Let's pause a moment and sense how your belly, heart, and muscles feel when you say the words:

Safe. I am safe.

And yet the world we live in doesn't always feel safe. I imagine each of us could easily make a personal list of ways that we feel endangered, worried, or even just unsure in our day-to-day lives. Yet even amidst these outward challenges, there is a kind of safety that we can feel in our bodies and in our minds that satisfies our deepest yearnings for security. And it is as close as the hand we extend to hold the hand of another.

We are literally built to be in warm, receptive relationships—it is rooted in our DNA. And yet, so much in our culture and our personal history can pull us away from this ever-present possibility. Because I lived so much of my life in the shadow of these cultural expectations and early attachment experiences that were painful, it took a lot of work to move away from what felt familiar for me and lean in to relationships that can heal both of these profound wounds.

I wrote my first book, *Anxiously Attached*, to help others with attachment wounds similar to mine find more fulfilling relationships. I was experiencing healing in that area and wanted to share it. In the years since, my own growth has continued, and I've realized that many of us have a variety of significant wounds from childhood that affect all our relationships. The impulse to share what I'm learning and experiencing is the foundation for *Safe*.

For each of us, our inner felt sense of how safe or unsafe we are comes from a lifetime of relational experiences. Our earliest connections, beginning even in the womb, teach us what to expect from those who are closest to us. These lessons run deep, forming a strong felt sense of whether people will be safe for us or whether they will be distant, aloof, anxious, upset, or downright dangerous. Then throughout our lives, we continue to meet and form attachments with many other people—teachers, relatives, romantic partners, friends—those who care for us and those who hurt us. We each have a complicated tangle of relational experiences that influence our inner sense of what is safe and what is not.

Beyond how nourishing or wounding our attachments have been, those of us living in Western culture have also been shaped by the values and expectations that are baked into what our society considers "the right way to live." Many of the messages we receive tell us that independence, self-reliance, self-regulation, self-care, and success are the hallmarks of maturity and health. And as a result, disconnection and judgment can begin very early in our lives. After all, our parents have been touched by the values of our society, too. When we're little, we're praised for achieving developmental milestones. We hear our parents say proudly, "My son walked at nine months." "My daughter could sort by color when she was two years old." They beam if we succeed and shrink away if we haven't met the standard. As children, we begin to feel that we are being measured and found pleasing or wanting according to these somewhat arbitrary markers. By the time we're moving toward adulthood, the expectation is that we will work hard and achieve goals in many areas of our lives. The unique beauty and gifts of each person can get lost in this sea of performance and competition. Living this way is the opposite of safe.

Because these demands keep us moving so fast and with such urgency, we often lose touch with our deepest yearning to slow down and savor safe, warm connection with others. British psychiatrist, literary scholar, philosopher, and neuroscientist Iain McGilchrist has spent decades unraveling the mysterious relationship between the two hemispheres of our brains. It isn't quite what we have been taught to think—that the right hemisphere controls creativity and the left focuses on logic. Instead, according to McGilchrist, it is like having two people in our brains who see and live in the world differently. The right is about connecting to the living experience of this moment (where we can find safety in relationships), while the tendency of the left is to shift away from this aliveness or any emotional struggle in order to organize our experience and focus on making things happen in the world (leading us to lose connection with the moment and each other). Both ways of experiencing are important, but *most* important is the relationship between the two. This matters to us because we have become an overwhelmingly left-dominant society, giving rise to an epidemic of traumatic loneliness. My own attachment wounds and propensity to remain in my left-brain hideout had me living at breakneck speed for many, many years. And then a romantic relationship forced me to face these wounds straight on.

There was nothing like that first hug. I remember the embrace like it was yesterday. When we met after weeks of talking on the phone, he immediately felt like "home" to me. It was as if a big sigh of relief came over my whole body. I could finally rest. Escaping into his arms and heart, it felt like we were meant to travel this life together. I don't believe I took in the significance of the word "escape" at that time. It would be almost two years before I realized he was providing me refuge and a hiding place from the pain and fear I was not yet ready to face.

As time passed, our love for each other increased and our relationship began to push us further and further in the direction of emotional intimacy. This progression is just what is supposed to happen. At this point, as in all close relationships, our early attachment patterns began to surface, inviting us to work on the ways we were beginning to struggle with each other. I sensed that my growing dependence on him was challenging for him, just as I struggled with his avoidant behaviors when he started shutting down, running away, and ignoring me. These intertwined dynamics where one person runs toward their partner, while the other person gets scared and runs away—two people who are never finding each other, never able to sustain long periods of connection—are often referred to as trauma bonding or the anxious-avoidant dance. Some spiritual communities refer to these dynamics as two individuals finding their "twin flames," romanticizing the patterns that can keep two people trapped for years. If you're familiar with any of these terms, then you likely have been in a relationship that has felt tremendously unsafe for you. Perhaps you were never quite clear why the relationship was so painful.

As I would soon learn, one person's painful early memories can awaken the other person's painful early memories. Of course, my partner felt like "home" for me. Beneath the instant passion, he was also carrying the patterns of what my earlier experiences of attachment felt like. When he got scared, he shut me out and ignored me, something I had experienced with both my parents. Initially, we were like two wounded children rushing toward each other, hoping for the other to fill the holes in us, only to gradually find out that neither of us had what the other needed because of our own wounds. My disappointment shattered the dream of perfection I had been living in.

In this book, we will trace how attachment wounds can surface and discover tools that can help you both uncover their origins and seek healing. The process is akin to peeling back layers of experience to uncover the insecure attachment experiences in your life that may have led you to develop protective behaviors, like running away or throwing yourself into work—anything to prevent the old pain and fear from rising to the surface. What I learned from my own experience and have since been able to share with my clients is that—as painful as the relationship was—one of my partner's actual roles in my life was to be the important and necessary catalyst for my true healing, and my hope is that you, too, will find a pathway to healing within the pages of this book.

Our Brains and Relationships

Sometimes the right person comes to us exactly when we need them. Around the time that my relationship was unraveling, I happened to hear about Bonnie Badenoch's *The Heart of Trauma*, a book that weaves attachment, trauma, and relational neuroscience together. I had been reading a fair amount about neuroscience before this, but Bonnie's book felt different. There was a softness to her words that touched something deeper in me. I believe I was already feeling some sense of safety because of the warm acceptance at the heart of her work. In the process, I was learning something very important through this experience. So often we hear that if we are able to heal, we will begin to feel safe. While that is true, perhaps it is more important to know that finding safety also comes as the prelude and foundation of healing. I got in touch with her, and she has become my mentor along this path. With Bonnie, I felt seen for the first time in my life. My interactions with her are profound because she shows up in all her wisdom, but also in such a present and compassionate way. When I was deep in pain, it was as if her mere presence gave me the courage to continue my healing journey—and I could sense that I needed to be around that more. My system was yearning for such calm, safe people.

The other side of feeling such safety is that I became vulnerable to memories from childhood. They started to come alive in me so that I could heal and integrate them, and at the same time brought big bouts of fear and pain to the surface. It was challenging but also felt essential. I found I was developing a new sense of agency and decided that no matter what was going on in my outer world, I was going to show up and continue to stay curious about what was coming up in my inner world. Most of all, I knew I had the right support to heal my deepest attachment pains and patterns. I began to widen the circle with more and more people who could support me in this journey. I came to call these people anchors, and throughout this book we will speak much more about how to find your own anchors and their role in healing.

Some people are able to make the journey toward healing together. But both people have to be willing. One of my clients yearned to reconcile with her mother, but years of alcoholism had rendered her mom unable to even consider trying to mend the broken bond. Something similar happened with my partner. When I approached him about doing this work together, he told me that he wanted a fantasy relationship, to stay in the early stage that felt like magic, not in the real one that required intense work. I knew there was no going back to the early times when we were simply lost in each other. As I was coming to understand it, I knew I didn't want to repeat this pattern with anyone ever again. It is important to say that none of this is intended to blame him. He loved me to the best of his ability. I truly believe that. But the repeating of painful dynamics is a tragic situation that so many of us live through again and again.

This is where doing *the work* with other people comes in. Our culture believes that independence and self-reliance are the gold standard for healthy maturity. Nothing could be further from the truth. As the brilliant American psychologist and researcher Stephen Porges says, "Connection is a biological imperative." For us humans, safety comes from warm, receptive connection. We simply cannot survive without it. Relational neuroscience describes how our system yearns for connection and that we are hyperaware when it is being offered to us—and also in those times when, sadly, it is not on offer. Porges is the father of what he calls the *polyvagal theory*. His work is all about the autonomic nervous system (ANS for short) and how it responds to connection and disconnection. Drawing on Porges's work, in the following pages we will explore our biological need for connection, and how a greater understanding of how our ANS works can help us to heal.

The ability to picture what is happening within our brains can help stabilize us and support us, confirming that we are headed in the right direction. As we take this journey together, the science will guide us, reassure us, and help us understand how we have been wounded and what begins to happen as we heal.

How to Make This Book Your Own

As I have said, having the warm support of others is so important on this path, and as you move through this book, I will be with you each step of the way. You will find meditations and reflections throughout. I have recorded versions of them so we can practice them together; you can find them separately at jessicabaumlmhc .com/safe-meditations. You may also find it very helpful to keep a journal nearby. As you read, memories and insights may come to you, and writing them down will help you begin to understand your life's attachment story. In the back of the book there is a section called Wisdom Notes, which will provide a little more information about the science. We will also talk at length about the importance of finding your *anchors*—people in your life who have the capacity to hold space for you. I will also introduce you to the possibility of having what Patty Wipfler, founder of Hand in Hand Parenting, calls *listening partners*, those precious people in our lives who have the ability to just listen and hold space for us rather than try to fix us. Sometimes, when the pain is especially deep, it can also be very important to seek the help of a therapist. As our powerful attachment stories make themselves known, we may be surprised by how much we begin to feel. I encourage you to get this extra support anytime you need it. I was incredibly fortunate to work with my own therapist, Jo, and I will tell you more about our work together in the pages that follow.

Let's take a quick stroll through the chapters ahead. Part 1, "Searching for Safety," lays the foundation for the work we'll be doing together. We will explore early attachment, tracing the lasting contribution parents and other caregivers have in our lives in terms of how safe or unsafe we feel in the world. We'll also explore the kinds of safe, nurturing relationships that make deep healing possible. I call these wonderful people *anchors* because—like the moorings that keep a ship firmly tethered to safe harbor—they give us a sense of coming home and settling into a felt sense of security. We will also explore the protective strategies we develop to keep us from drowning in the internal pain and fear we experience when our attachment wounds are awakened. Some of us overeat. Some of us bury ourselves in work, social media, drugs, isolation, and all the myriad ways our creative inner world can provide. Slowly, gently, we'll get to know these adaptive patterns we might call *protectors*. Taking them out of the shadows and bringing them into light is a crucial step in the healing process. We'll end part 1 by considering the paradox of our own vulnerability. This tender state can be terrifying, but it also opens the door to healing.

Part 2, "Coming Home to Our Bodies," forms the heart of this work. Each of the three chapters in this section centers around specific practices for deepening into the work of healing from the attachment wounds we are carrying. In chapter 4, "The Eternally Present Past," we'll practice something called *interoception*, which is the ability to listen to the sensations happening all the time in our bodies. The sense of our hearts expanding with joy. The uneasiness in our bellies when something scares us. This skill is so important because the traumatic memories that need healing are held in our bodies: bellies, hearts, autonomic nervous systems, muscles, even our skin. Each has its own way of *remembering* our experiences and then reminding us of the felt sense and meaning of each one. They are all communicating at once, and together they make up what is called *implicit memory*. The most important thing about this kind of remembering is that these old experiences arise in our bodies and are experienced as if they are happening right now, shaping our perception of the present moment. With practice, you will begin to notice that your body is always talking to you, making you aware of whatever is waking up inside you.

In chapter 5, "Healing Our Younger Selves," with our interoception gradually gaining strength, we'll begin to listen for the embodied voices of our younger selves, from infancy up into adulthood. When we go inside to do this work, we will likely find memories filled with joy and loving care along with those that carry different shades of fear and pain. The experiences of warmth and security will become part of your anchoring resources, reminding you of the power of close connection to heal those parts of yourself that may have felt abandoned.

In chapter 6, "Healing the Patterns That Keep Us Stuck," we'll explore how patterns that formed in our childhood relationships often resurface in our adult relationships. Everyone with whom we have an emotionally meaningful connection in our lives, no matter the quality of that bond, imprints themselves in our implicit memory.

Our teachers, neighbors, siblings, friends, work companions—all of these people come to live inside us, and the things they taught us about connection, about what feels safe and not safe, can influence how close or disconnected we feel in our adult relationships. Through these interactions, we develop a *wheel of attachment possibilities* rather than just a single style. We'll spend slow, important time exploring how this has been for us. How do we expect people to be with us? And, just as importantly, how do we respond as people become close to us? How do the relational patterns from our early insecure relationships get re-created in our adult relationships? How can we become aware of these patterns so that we can heal them?

While this process may bring up a lot of pain and fear, when each part is welcomed with tenderness and a wish to offer whatever comfort is needed, a kind of deep joy also begins to well up. I will share a lot of stories side by side with the science. My story. Other people's experiences. (All names and histories have been changed to protect each person's privacy.) I trust these will also be your companions along the way, telling the truth about the difficulty of this process while providing comfort and hope for the remarkable healing that is possible for each of us.

At the beginning of part 3, "Living in Heartfelt Connection," in chapter 7, "Knowing When to Stay—and When It's Time to Go," we will sift through our experiences and examine what might draw us into relationships in which we try to take care of a wounded person at the expense of our own healing. We'll explore how we can know when people in these relationships don't have the capacity to heal together, so it might be time to leave. Our hope here is to amplify compassion for people who suffer in these terrible ways because there is often so much judgment and rejection of them when none of their behaviors are their fault. It is equally important to have compassion for ourselves as we seek relationships that offer mutual nourishment.

In chapter 8, "What Happens When We Heal?," we will celebrate the signs that we are slowly lifting the weight of trauma off our shoulders. We'll come back to what the research shows us about the new neural circuitry that forms when our wounds heal, so we can picture the beautiful changes unfolding in our embodied brains. Our expanding felt sense of safety gives us new strengths to bring into relationships. One of the most important is something called *response flexibility*, which means that when something distressing happens, our system will let us slow down enough to not react quickly, but instead to consider, become curious, and stay connected with our partner. That one change can alter the trajectory of a relationship.

Chapter 9, "Reaching Your Safe Harbor," is this book's *harbor and anchor*. Here we will reflect with gratitude on what is possible as we continue with this work. By now you may be sensing that safety is both an inside and an outside job. Our inner healing begins to resonate in our connections with others. Kindness becomes more common than criticism. Warm curiosity becomes more natural than judgment. Cooperation feels better than competition. We're still human beings with all our frailties and tendencies, but when we've gained a sense of safety and belonging, we can find our way back from the stumbles more quickly so that rupture followed by repair becomes a way of life.

At the root of this process is the deepening compassion that healing brings. The shifts in our felt sense of safety and connection are accompanied by an expanding wisdom that understands and feels how wounded people wound others. If we aren't safe for each other, it's because our inner world hasn't experienced enough care and belonging. The wonder is that in the warm embrace of non-judgmental holding, we will find that everything we need to be able to heal arises in the space between us. Bit by bit, we become anchored and can say, "I am safe. We are safe together." Let's begin.

1

SEARCHING FOR SAFETY

CHAPTER 1

THE POWER OF CONNECTION

don't feel safe!" I shouted at my partner as I tried desperately to catch my breath. It felt like a cord that once connected us had snapped.

"What do you mean, you don't feel safe?" he asked, staring at me with a detached look on his face. I didn't know how to respond—all I could do was repeat the words over and over: *"I don't feel safe."*

My partner was clearly confused by my suggestion that something dangerous was happening between us. After all, he was not physically abusing me or threatening any violence. He wasn't even yelling at me. The truth is that I was confused myself, as there really was no clear evidence that I was in an unsafe environment.

What I did feel was his distance. Instead of "we are together," I felt a cold, frightening sense of "I am alone." The firm ground and foundation of safety is connection, and as that dropped away, the sensations radiating through my body spoke the frightening truth.

I didn't know it at the time, but my partner was taking stimulants to dull the pain of grief. Just a couple of months earlier, his father had passed away, and in addition to absorbing this terrible loss, he was facing the overwhelming demands of taking over the family business. When we feel unsafe, our systems begin to look for adaptive ways to protect ourselves. We fight. We flee. We freeze. We collapse. Or we reach out for help.

The protective responses that come most naturally to us are the ones we learned in early childhood and have continued to rely on throughout our lives. Drawing on a lifetime of watching his father, my partner became a workaholic, literally taking flights all over the country for business meetings while pouring stimulants into his body in an attempt to outrun the inner chaos and fear. Fighting and fleeing at the same time, he had no felt sense of safety—but because he was not falling into an intolerable pit of grief and helplessness, his inner state of turmoil was not obvious from the outside.

In response to his behaviors, I also drew on a lifetime of experience. Just as I had done with my parents as a child, I ran toward my partner, desperate for safety. But he didn't feel safe enough inside himself to connect with me—instead he just shut down and moved away from me. Feeling alone, I became angry, but this only caused him to turn away even more. When I eventually collapsed and lay motionless on the couch, he was unable to make any move toward me. This feeling of having nowhere to turn was the most devastating of all, awakening the intense feelings of isolation and abandonment I had experienced from my earliest attachments.

4

We were two people who I believe still loved each other, but our wounds from the past made it difficult for us to come back to enough safety to reconnect. Where before there had been closeness and a deep feeling of being secure in our love, now there was only a lack of eye contact, anger, shutting down, separation, and silence. As these moments in which there was such a great distance between us became more and more frequent, the feeling of danger in our relationship grew, because the threat we fear most is loss of connection.

Relational neuroscience tells us that feelings of abandonment in our current lives can awaken the ghosts of similar losses we experienced when we were young. We call these early injuries *developmental traumas* or *attachment wounds*. Knowing what I do about his history, I can imagine how the child inside my partner was experiencing emotions that had been awakened by our current circumstances. He hadn't had much safety as a kid. His mother was highly anxious and his father was very detached and busy, traveling much of the time for work. My partner was one of those children who tried to stay connected by meeting his mother's needs at the expense of acknowledging his own. With no one available to listen to him, he never learned how to talk about what was going on inside him. Everything stayed locked away, unseen by anyone. As he got older, he developed strategies to avoid intimacy. Using substances to self-medicate, he protected himself by running away from other people's pain.

I had a different experience. For me, the unimaginable loss of closeness with my partner was bringing back embodied memories of the deep abandonment of my own childhood with a father who turned to substances to dull his pain and a mother whose challenging professional life meant she had very little time for me. I'm someone who has a strong need for warm attachment, and with no one available for connection, I became very sad and anxious. When my parents were unable to respond to this, I began to look around and saw that independence and self-reliance were highly valued qualities. I poured my attention into performing the role of self-sufficient girl, pushing down my vital and tender young need for connection. At times, this strong and independent part of me was an adequate protector, but when my partner's wounds caused him to abandon me, the anxiety and grief of my childhood were unleashed, amplifying the anguish of losing him.

What happens to us when we are small impacts how safe we feel now. We come into this world literally reaching out for connection. This need is wired into our systems at the most profound level. In fact, our craving for and reliance upon others is one of the most fundamentally true things about us humans. Renowned psychiatrist and researcher Stephen Porges says, "Connection is a biological imperative, meaning, it is vital and we can not survive without it." When we are brand-new to this world, we yearn for warm eyes and tender skin-to-skin touch from parents who welcome us with a sweet curiosity about this marvelous being who has just arrived in their lives. When we are met this way, we sense that the world is a safe place for us. But so many parents aren't able to receive us in this way because of their own wounds, often from their early childhoods.

In the 1950s, researcher John Bowlby began writing about what happens to babies whose parents create a loving and safe environment for them and to others whose parents were not able to be fully present for them. This led to the field of attachment, which

established three major categories to describe the connection between children and their parents or caregivers and how it impacts
children as they grow into adulthood and for the rest of their
lives: *secure*, *anxious ambivalent*, and *avoidant*. Later on, Mary Main and Erik Hesse
added a fourth category—*disorganized*.
Here, we want to just sample something
about each way of connecting in order to

> The threat we
> fear most is loss
> of connection.

begin to give you a sense of the different experiences you may have
had on this spectrum. We will go into this more later, but suffice to
say here that *attachment styles are by no means fixed* because each of us
has experiences of more than one style depending on the many particular relationships we have had. Throughout this book, we will
explore together how your own attachment system works, but we will
go into it in great depth in chapters 4, 5, and 6. For this first exploration of how these four ways of attaching may show up for you, we will
paint a picture of a parent-child attachment pair. It is important to
acknowledge that each parent-child pair in the world is unique, so
we're just giving a general idea here. The main thing to focus on as
you read these general descriptions of the major attachment styles
is whether you feel a strong resonance with one or more patterns.

SECURE

Earlier in this chapter, we talked a little bit about the *secure attachment* provided by warm, safe parents whose own inner world is

mostly settled, enabling them to be welcoming and receptive in relationship with us. They are *warmly curious* about us and reflect our uniqueness. Parents are literally building the neural circuitry of a baby's brain, so their inner experience of safety becomes ours. Being in their presence means that we are then wired to expect that we will be supported and cared for, that *the world is a good place.*

◎

ANXIOUS AMBIVALENT

Sadly, for some of our parents, their experience in early life has left them with an inner feeling that the world is an unpredictable place, that they aren't safe. They may feel anxious and sometimes get angry, and almost always desperately need someone else to comfort and support them. They aren't able to regularly offer their babies a place to be settled and held because that was not what they received. Sometimes they're available and sometimes not. This scares their little ones, who don't know what to expect next. *Loss of connection* is always just around the corner. Although the parents don't mean to, they are neurobiologically implanting their anxiety in their children, who often adapt by abandoning their own needs to try to take care of their parents. "If only I can make my mommy calm and happy, she will be with me." We then grow up with an enormous sensitivity to the feelings of others and little expectation that our own needs matter. We live in constant fear that we will be abandoned as we were in childhood. The researchers call this pattern *anxious ambivalent attachment*, something with which I am very familiar.

AVOIDANT

At the other end of the spectrum, we find *avoidant attachment.* Parents who are anxious are overwhelmed by their emotions, while avoidant parents have adapted to the pain in their lives by turning away from emotion, focusing instead on work or other areas of life where they can find a sense of accomplishment and control. In order to create distance from their feelings, they view the world through their left hemispheres. From that perspective, goals and tasks matter more than relationships, and criticism and judgment of others (and themselves) come naturally. Having disconnected from any feelings of sadness and pain, they are blind to the emotions of others, too. For their babies, this can feel like complete abandonment. In our earliest years, we are all right-hemisphere relational creatures, always seeking warm, responsive people, so to have avoidant parents is to feel as though we don't exist much of the time. Later on, when we are no longer babies and can speak, we might say to our parent, "I'm sad," only to be met by bewilderment, cold eyes, anger, or even a turned back. My clients who experienced growing up with avoidant parents often use the word "annihilation" to describe the vast black hole inside them.

In an anxious family, the child often adapts by becoming the caretaker. In an avoidant family, the safest adaptation is to show no emotional vulnerability and to perform well. Having given up any hope for warmth or safety in their relationship with their parents, they turn to other pursuits that might at least earn their approval—

good grades, perfect behavior. Emotional needs are set aside. As a result, their young brains are wired to be out of touch with their emotional needs. Tragically, our success-drunk culture rewards this kind of adaptation, leading to the current epidemic of hyper-independence and loneliness.

DISORGANIZED

With anxious and avoidant attachment, there are at least some ways to stay partially connected with our parents. But the researchers noticed that some children simply fell apart when offered connection with anyone. These babies became *disorganized*, making frantic gestures or simply collapsing. I have experienced these feelings at times and have come to understand that they occur when there is no one I can orient to, no safe place to land. If I turned toward my parents, they were unresponsive and lost in their own pain. If I turned away from them, I fell into the terror of aloneness, feeling shattered inside. Fortunately, these were isolated experiences that left pockets of disorganization while most of my daily life was some combination of anxious and avoidant.

It's pretty common these days for someone to ask, "What's your attachment style?" I'm grateful that now there is so much more awareness about the power of our early attachments and how they shape the way we currently relate. But those first connections are just the beginning of the experiences that shape our expectations about how relationships will be for us. Every emotionally meaningful connection leaves its mark. So rather than asking you to identify your attachment style, we're going to explore how we develop what we might call a *wheel of attachment*. Mine includes experiences of security and anxiety with my mother, avoidance and anxiety with my father, security with my grandmother, and moments of such profound abandonment that I sometimes became disorganized. Depending on who I'm with or what's happening around me, I can drop into any of the adaptive responses I developed in this kaleidoscope of relationships.

I have worked with so many clients who have parents with different attachment styles. Often, one parent has more anxiety while the other has more of a tendency to hide away behind a newspaper or with busy tasks while both of them also offer experiences of warm security. We'll be deeply exploring how it was for you in chapter 5, although you already may be getting some hints just by reading this. If that's the case, jotting down some notes in your journal may be very helpful.

> Every emotionally meaningful connection leaves its mark.

THE ROOTS OF SECURITY

As we begin this journey, it's helpful to start picturing what types of experiences can lead to secure attachment and what factors might contribute to insecurity. After decades of studying the autonomic nervous system (ANS), the part of our nervous system that responds automatically to internal and external conditions, Stephen Porges developed the polyvagal theory to describe the adaptive way our ANS continually responds to changes in circumstances. According to the polyvagal theory, our ANS constantly scans our internal and external environment to rapidly sense risk and safety, causing shifts in our autonomic state without our conscious awareness. Porges helps us understand the primary quality that allows parents to foster a sense of safety for their offspring and thus create a secure foundation for attachment. This key ingredient is *presence*. It may sound strange that love isn't at the top of the list, but our parents may love us very much and still not be able to actually be present with us because of their own wounds.

What we mean by presence is their ability to see us and receive us *as we are*, from moment to moment, with warmth, curiosity, tenderness, and often delight. *They are more interested in finding out who we are than in needing us to be a certain way.* This is the key. When they miss the mark in their response to us, they usually notice it and often work to reconnect, even if it takes a while.

What is happening within the parent when they are able to offer true presence? Stephen Porges has coined a phrase to describe this state—the parent is having a *neuroception of safety*. Neuroception is a subconscious process that allows our bodies to sense whether we are feeling safe or not. It's an automatic process that operates outside of conscious thought and is generated by parts of the brain that evolved before the conscious mind. When we say *felt experience*, we mean that it is showing up in our bodies—in our bellies, in our muscles, in our chest, even in our skin. This inner assessment of safe/not safe is happening in nanoseconds all the time. Much faster than conscious thought. Our bodies are constantly whispering to us, "You are safe" or "You are not safe." We are social creatures who find our safety with each other, so the central question of our whole system is "Are you with me?" When a parent is able to offer this sense of true safety to their child, it builds a foundation of security that the child can take with them as they move through life.

Neuroception is made up of three experiences that are always happening within us:

1. What past experiences are awake inside us right now? Something that feels safe? Something that feels unsafe? Our past experiences are stored deep in the recesses of our memory, held as sensations in our bodies—in our bellies, hearts, muscles, and more. Whatever is awake within us influences our internal sense of how safe or unsafe we feel in this moment, no matter how long ago it occurred.

2. Who/what is in our environment right now? Does this experience or person feel safe or unsafe?

3. Who is accompanying me? Is there a trustworthy person by my side or not? Or can I summon an awareness of a safe person in my life, a relationship I've internalized that I can draw on in this moment to help me feel safe?

In the time it took you to read these three short descriptions, your system had a constant stream of shifting neuroceptions, so many, in fact, that there is no way to track all of them consciously.

Regardless of what we may currently be feeling or doing, our neuroception is always telling us the truth about how safely connected we feel right now, and adapting our thoughts, feelings, behaviors, and relationships in response. For instance, when I would awaken in the middle of the night to find that my partner wasn't in bed with me, before I even had time to think about what this might mean, my heart would begin racing and my muscles would tense as I prepared to leap out of bed. As I breathed rapidly from high in my chest, my eyes would dart around the dark room looking for him, and eventually I would call out his name. His absence had awakened old fears of abandonment, generating a powerful neuroception of danger that quickly entered my consciousness, leading to these feelings of terror welling up inside me. The sudden awareness of past experiences of being left alone coupled with his very real absence in the moment—that there was no one physically there to help me hold this fear—raised all the alarms in my body. As soon as I would call out to him and he'd answer that he had just gone to the bathroom, my system would immediately settle back into a neuroception of safety. I wasn't abandoned. My trustworthy person was nearby.

When we are having a neuroception of safety, our ANS activates what Porges calls the *social engagement system*, which allows us to connect with those around us. It softens our bellies, relaxes our muscles (especially around our eyes), gives our voices a particular quality that signals safety, and assists us in listening deeply without judgment. This is our ANS's preferred state because our whole system wants to be in warm connection with others.

What might this look like between parents and their newborn? I am a new mom with my infant son in my arms. Inside me, I have the long-ago experience of my mother looking lovingly at me (safe). I feel comfortably at home with supportive people around me (safe). In this moment, my best friend is gazing lovingly at the two of us (safe). My baby can look up into my eyes and find the safe haven of me being truly present to him. In this moment, my baby's little brain is being primed to expect the world to be a safe place in which he is a child who is loved and taken care of.

Then, as often happens, he becomes uncomfortable and begins to fuss and then cry. I may feel a little concerned because all this is new, but my inner world is filled with the felt sense of my own mom taking care of my needs, my outer world is consistently supportive, and my friend helps me tend to my little one. Even in the midst of this disturbance, all is still safe inside me. So even while my baby cries, he is taking in that safety. Once we discover he's hungry, calm returns. And his system is being shaped to expect that when something goes wrong, it can be set right again. This is the pattern of secure attachment rooted in parents' ability to be present enough of the time.

That's an important phrase: "enough of the time." Every parent will get upset, angry, frustrated, confused, and anxious at moments, having temporarily left behind the neuroception of safety. Recognizing that this is happening, especially if we can do that without judgment because we realize it is just part of being human, is the first step to finding a way back to warm connection. There are no perfect parents. In fact, research by neuroscientist Ed Tronick tells us that we offer the accurate empathic relational response about 33 percent of the time, and the other 67 percent is what he calls "rupture and repair" referring to those moments in our relationships when conflict might arise but we are, eventually, able to come back together. (We'll explore this essential process more throughout this book and especially in chapter 8.) What a relief to not have to be perfect! In fact, these experiences of missing the mark and then restoring connection actually strengthen the safety and security in the relationship. Each of us has probably had many experiences as adults when things go sideways with someone we love, and then both find our way back to talk through the difficulty to connect with each other again. Trusting that you will eventually come together to talk things through and reconnect is one of the greatest gifts we can give each other.

When we are fortunate enough to have safe, warm early connections, several things happen easily, establishing us in secure attachment. Once we feel someone being truly *present* with us, the most natural thing is to make *contact*. Sometimes we lock eyes and look deeply; sometimes we make physical contact. It is as though we put down an anchor within each other. Even babies do this as they gaze for long moments with their mom and dad while relishing skin-to-skin contact in their parents' safe arms. A wonderful sense of refuge, of sanctuary is becoming deeply embedded.

And as we grow into adulthood, with these moments of truly seeing another person and, in turn, being seen by them, comes a quality of *reflection*. Our whole being is telling the other how wonderful they are, just as they are, and they, in response, are telling us

I see you, too. As we mirror each other, this state of joy becomes a part of who we are. Without these warm reflections, there is the tenuous sense of not being sure our inner state is real. We are so beautifully dependent on how others see us to discover who we are.

All of this need for connection with and affirmation from other humans is rooted in our parents' ability to be present with us as children. As we play at their feet when we are tiny and then onward as we venture farther and farther out into the world under their watchful gaze, their consistent presence in our lives satisfies our need for contact, reflection, responsiveness, and delight.

> Our whole system wants to be in warm connection with others.

If we are lucky, we get parents who can provide us with enough of a sense of safety to feel fundamentally good in the world. However, what I have learned from working with my clients is that many of their parents struggled with their own attachment wounds. One of my clients described feeling as a young child that her very young mother loved her deeply but that her own experiences from childhood had left her mother feeling alternately afraid of or disinterested in the responsibility of caring for her. With no one around to support her as a young single mother, she must have felt abandoned and alone. My client described to me how, when she would cry out for her mother, her mother would either look around in a distracted way or frantically try one thing after another to quiet her daughter's cries. It seemed part of my client's mother wanted to just put her down (avoidant), and part of her felt desperate to help her feel better (anxious). Meanwhile, my client's little body and brain were learning to expect that this world is not a safe place, that no one would be truly with her. A foundation of insecurity and fear had taken root that lingered in her inner world into adulthood. Our work together involved revisiting these feelings and helping her to find the love and support she needed in her relationships with her friends and family now to give her a sense of true safety in her life.

THE CONTINUING POWER OF ATTACHMENT

These earliest patterns of relating stay with us. If we grew up with a *felt sense* (a feeling in our bodies) that our needs are going to be met by our parents and caregivers, then as adults we will have a greater sense of safety and trust in others. As a result, we're likely to be pulled toward people who actually have the capacity to meet our needs, and we will be more able to meet theirs. For those of us who are securely attached, this happens automatically and fairly effortlessly.

For many of us, myself included and maybe you as well, since you picked up this book, our earliest connections didn't provide this security, so we often feel unsafe and confused, especially in close relationships. Because of what we learned so early in our lives about connection or lack thereof, we anticipate and are drawn to what we experienced as little ones. We have a tendency to go toward what is familiar.

If my earliest times included a sense that my closest people turned their backs on me, I will feel both agitated by and drawn toward people who ignore me. Both the pattern and the pain are familiar, and what's even more powerful is that this is all my system knows to expect.

If my childhood left me consumed by an anxious overfocus on those I looked to for care and love, I may well respond now by rushing toward those in need of support and regulation, abandoning my own needs to try to calm them. It's the only way I can imagine being close.

WHAT HAPPENS NEXT?

The good news is that we are never too old to heal our attachment wounds and change the quality of our relationships. Built right into our DNA are the yearning and capacity for warm, nourishing relationships. It is as though our system has been waiting all our lives for the right support to help us explore and heal the pain and fear of our early losses. These precious relationships will also become the bedrock for our emerging sense of security. Attachment is always a two-person process, both when it gives us a warm sense of trust in others and when it is filled with turned backs and anxious eyes. My hope for this book is that it becomes both a sanctuary and an encouragement for you to find those relationships that will become your anchors as we move through this healing together.

> We are never too old to heal our attachment wounds.

CHAPTER 2

FINDING YOUR ANCHORS

So much of our learning in this culture is about being independent, self-reliant, and more. As we are discovering, relational neuroscience tells us that we are built to thrive in a nest of warm relationships. Our own inner world already knows this, but we may have buried the knowing to become part of this disconnected society. Now we're finding out that in our safe interactions with others, we can touch and heal the attachment wounds we carry. These warm and present people are our anchors.

As I began to write this chapter, I looked up synonyms for "anchor." Let's see what happens in your body when you slowly read these words: moor, mainstay, support, root, tether, sanctuary, refuge, shelter, safe haven, oasis, *home*. Based on your past experiences of connection, anything might happen in your body in response to these words. There is no right or wrong feeling.

Our bodies speak the many truths of our varied experiences. Hearing these words for "anchor," we might feel a profound sadness in our chest and belly or become numb if what came to us in previous moments of need was no one being there. We might feel anger remembering a time when we sought a good listener but found only someone who wanted to offer advice. Or we might feel a deep settling as images and feelings of past moments of warm connection arise. As best we can, let's welcome all of our feelings as they roll through our bodies. We can come back to these words echoing the feeling of being anchored often to see how the way they touch us changes. In this chapter, we're going to explore the many ways anchors show up in our lives and how we can surround ourselves with more and more of them.

WELCOMING OUR INNER ANCHORS

We can begin by celebrating that we all have both inner and outer anchors. Let's first spend some time with the inner ones. Of the many gifts bestowed by our evolving brains, the one that is perhaps most life-giving is that the people, animals, and places that have held us and nourished us stay with us. They are permanent sources of hope, meaning, resilience, and support.

Neuroscience researcher Marco Iacoboni and his team discovered that the human brain contains mirror neurons, neural cells that respond in equal measure when we perform a certain task as when we simply observe the task being executed by others. These neurons pave the way for us to, as he says, "live within each other." Coupled with these mirror neurons, we have neural pathways, called *resonance circuits*, that are dedicated to this process of internalizing others. It isn't just that we consciously remember the actions and physical presence of those around us. We have the ability to actually *feel them with us* as a living part of our inner world. Let's pause and really get a sense of that. Science now shows that we take each other in and actually do live within each other.

Our inner anchors are those special people in our lives who live within us as a continuous source of care. They have a gift for being able to truly see us; they can also stay open and receptive when we share our pain, fear, and vulnerability. These anchors form the core of our inner refuge. Reading these words may bring certain people to your mind and heart—and may also awaken your body as a warmth arises in your chest, light fills your eyes, and waves of gratitude flow throughout your body. Like all of us, they are not perfect, but they are at home in their humanity and able to repair ruptures that may occur when things have gone awry in the relationship. Most important, they listen deeply rather than trying to fix us. They offer us a safe haven that allows our whole system to feel settled just by thinking of them.

Pause for Reflection

Let's take a moment to invite our anchors in and relish their presence. Think of a person or even an animal or a place that makes you feel safe and at home. What happens in your body when you think of them? Do you feel warmth in any areas of your body? Or perhaps just a feeling of deep peace all over your body? If you like, make a note in your journal about the sensations you feel when you think of this person, animal, or place.

When I was a little girl, I knew my mother loved me, but she was often overwhelmed and preoccupied with survival and her career, while my deeply wounded father struggled to be present with me at all. During this difficult time in my life, my mother's mother, whom we called Nonna, emerged as an unwavering anchor. She radiated warmth, providing the steady love and nurturing care that filled my childhood beginning from when I was about six and we moved to New Jersey near my grandparents. Nonna would pick up my sister and me after school on Fridays and we would spend the weekends in their tiny, cozy apartment. It was a haven, brimming with love and the aroma of Italian spices in the rich tomato sauce that was often simmering on the stove for hours. There was something about the combination of nourishing food and warm arms that filled me in a particular way. I was sick a lot in those days, possibly because of the constant stress at home, and Nonna gave me such reassuring care at those times, even singing to me.

As I'm writing this, I can feel her nearby. Along with all the loving care, I am remembering her strong old-school convictions about the way girls should behave. Even though her strictness irritated me at the time, her out-of-date protectiveness feels like part of her affectionate care for us now. She came into our lives at a most important moment when her presence could at least partially offset our father's neglect. It feels alarming to imagine how different my inner world would be now if she hadn't been there to soften the pain of the aloneness we were suffering during the week. The act of leaving her home on Sunday evenings brought on deep sobs as we returned to a world without that nurturing warmth and care.

For most of us, only a very few people have offered such thorough and continuous anchoring as Nonna did for my sister and me. Instead, many provide a mixture of different attachment experiences, some hurtful, some neutral, and some nurturing. As I've been reflecting on my own life for this book, it has become clear to me that even though my mother's anxiety and absorption in her career meant that most of the time she was not able to be a consistently safe, warm presence for me, we did have periods of our life that drew us together. The memories of connection with my mother that are the strongest for me came from our shared love of horseback riding. Our time at the stables with these magnificent creatures brought us close to each other, providing a sense of safe haven that I still cherish. In the midst of the everyday emptiness in my home, these moments gave me solace and stability. Now, whenever I encounter the earthy scent of a barn, I am drawn back to the felt sense of settling into warmth and goodness with my mother.

Even the most difficult relationships can offer us oases of welcome and care. My friend, whose father was critical of her throughout her childhood, can also feel how playful he was with her. Her body remembers his laughing, throwing her tiny self into the air, dancing with her to silly music, and relishing every little moment of

Fourth of July festivities. When these moments come back to her, the pain of his humiliating comments feels distant because of the way our inner world protects these precious relationships inside. Our systems store painful and frightening memories in a way that keeps them from overwhelming us all the time, while integrating nurturing experiences in a way that they are easily accessible to us.

⊚

ACCESSING OUR INNER ANCHORS

We take in the living presence of so many relationships over the course of our lives. Once we have taken people into our hearts, we have the ability to access their presence and their energy when sad or stressful times come to us. Right now, as we are just beginning to walk this path together, it will be helpful to invite some of these people, animals, and places into conscious awareness. They don't have to be parents. A teacher, a pet, a friend, or a place in nature may come to mind. Working with clients for many years, I have heard about childhood pets who were the primary source of unconditional love. Some people summon the sanctuary of a forest or a garden or the seaside or the wind in the trees.

One of my clients told me these memories feel like snow globes to her, each with its own warm and nurturing scene inside. She said she can visit them whenever she begins to feel overwhelmed by the pain of her childhood, allowing her body to rest in safety for at least a few minutes. If we can tap into times in our lives when we felt seen and held, it will help us to connect back into the essence of that kind of attentive care. The early chapters of this book are meant to provide a sturdy foundation for the work ahead. Coming into living contact with these internal anchors is such an important part of our preparation. Because so much of this internalization process happens below conscious awareness, we may not have had any reason to attend to those who live inside us. Part of our work will be to become more conscious of this rich universe of relationships. There will be many opportunities to deepen this awareness in the chapters ahead. Once we begin to pay attention, it seems that more and more of our nurturers come forward to be known.

Practice for Reconnecting with Our Inner Sources of Warm Support and Safety

To help you consciously access and draw upon the energy of the inner anchors in your life, let's begin to gently recall and embrace the warmth and care from both beings and places that have offered you solace and support. Following this practice, you may want to write down your reflections in your journal. Or you may have found a trustworthy companion or two to share your discoveries with, or even do the practices together.

1. Begin by finding a quiet place where you feel comfortable and protected. Let yourself feel that it's time to slow down as best you can. Many of us

have been running so fast for so long that slowing down is quite a challenge.

2. Close your eyes and let your mind wander back to past moments in your life when you felt truly seen, supported, and held. Allow these memories to surface naturally. Remember, these caring presences need not be just from people. They can be pets, places in nature, or any entity that has provided you comfort and steady support.

3. As these memories and feelings arise, visualize each being in whatever form they arrive forming a circle around you. Picture a teacher's encouraging smile, the warmth of a pet's presence, the serene beauty of a favorite place in nature—each adding their felt sense of safety and goodness to your circle.

4. Focus on the feeling each memory brings up in your body. Notice any shifts or sensations as you allow yourself to be enveloped in their presence. Like the client who envisioned her memories as snow globes, imagine holding each warm and nurturing scene in your hands.

5. Silently or aloud, express your gratitude to each of your anchors for the support and care they've provided. Acknowledge their role in your life and the comfort they continue to offer you.

6. Spend a few minutes just resting in the presence of these sources of love and safety. When you're ready, bring your attention back to the present moment. Take a few deep breaths and notice how you feel.

CONNECTING WITH OUR OUTER ANCHORS

The next big question is: "Who are my anchoring people now? Who listens to me without judging me and without immediately jumping in to fix me or the situation?"

When I ask clients this question, a surprising number have said, "No one." Most often, it isn't because people don't care, but because our left-dominant culture has trained us to see problems and look for solutions, neglecting to pause to actually hear each other. This urge to fix has almost become a reflex. I can hear it in myself, that murmuring voice in the background that is dreaming up ways to help even while my friend is pouring her heart out to me. I have to corral my attention so I can come back to the present moment and settle into fully listening from my heart. Our left hemispheres will tell us we aren't doing enough if we "just" listen, but it turns out that the best doing is being fully present, creating an oasis of safety so that the other person can hear themselves more deeply, feel the healing wash of warm comfort, and then come into contact with their own inner wisdom. Not that any of this is easy. We learn it from receiving it and then practicing, practicing, practicing.

My friend Alan is that anchoring presence for me. He doesn't seem to feel the inner urge to fix things. I would sense it if he did. Instead, he provides an accepting and compassionate ear and heart, taking in all my emotions with his steadiness and care. He seems to effortlessly stay open in a way that feels so safe to me. This makes it possible for me to process what has happened, at my own pace, as I continue to navigate the complex layers of past and present heartbreak. This may sound odd, but Alan doesn't try to make me feel better. He is not a fixer. As he sits with me, the anguish may soften or intensify, but no matter what comes, he holds and witnesses it, changing something so fundamental. He is with me in experiences where I have always been alone. The feeling of being "with" is the magic.

Another quality of anchoring comes from my therapist, Jo. These days, most therapy training is about assessing and fixing, so it has been supremely important for me to find someone who is able to be fully present without their own agenda. Jo has helped me cultivate a deep sense of safety so that I can explore my childhood wounds, trusting I will be caught and held. I can get so young with her that the very roots of my developmental trauma are unearthed to receive what I have always needed.

Because of my own wounds, it has taken me a while to recognize what I actually need to feel safe and held by others. Having someone either ignore what I am saying or tell me I am handling a situation in the wrong way is mostly what I knew growing up—it felt familiar. Even though my body protested with an upset stomach and a tight chest, I accepted these responses from friends and family members as they felt "normal" to me, just the way relationships are. It took some time to see that what I really need from my anchors is to just sit with me and be fully present, without feeling the need to judge or advise me.

As we have discussed, the quality of our current relationships is influenced by the expectations we developed when we were small. Some of us were fortunate to internalize secure parents, allowing us to move through this complex and difficult world feeling generally safe and calm. We anticipate people being supportive and have a tendency to attract those kinds of people into our lives. The kind of care we received early on is internalized not just through the presence of our parents. We also have neurochemical support in the form of a rich supply of receptors for oxytocin and serotonin. Our path to locating outer anchors is often smooth.

In contrast, many of us with insecure attachment wounds didn't have the opportunity to internalize secure people in our earlier years. We took in parents who were more frightened, critical, or absent. This left us to grow up with less of a feeling of internal stability and an impoverished neurochemical system. Relationships that leave us feeling unseen or wounded are familiar to us, so we often have a tendency to draw in others who follow the patterns we learned as little ones. This was certainly my experience.

Fortunately, history isn't destiny. Armed with the knowledge of relational neuroscience and the support of this book, we can begin to look for and lean into relationships with people who are able to be present with us, without judgment and without an agenda to fix us. Even one supportive relationship can set us on this path.

One of my clients decided she was going to see if there was a trustworthy person or two among her current friends. She began to listen to how her friends usually talked with one another. There was a lot of teasing, a lot of suggestions for doing things differently, and very little sense of depth in their conversations. But she also really liked these women. So, finding some bravery deep within her, she began to risk telling them the truth about how the conversations felt to her. She shared how lonely she felt when she thought about telling them what was making her sad because she was afraid they would tease or correct her. She asked them if they were feeling that, too. While several of them said they liked the lighthearted way things were, two of them took her aside and said, yes, that's how they were feeling, too. This was the beginning of two meaningful friendships that carried them all to a deeper level of safe and healing connection. We celebrated her courage and her discovery that such relationships are possible in her life. It may be that our relationship paved the way for her wanting more of this in her daily experience. And it is my hope that this book will be that for you.

History isn't destiny.

FINDING YOUR LISTENING PARTNER

One of the most beneficial ways to deepen into healing is to have fellow travelers on this path, what I think of as *co-anchors*, practicing and learning together. This is what the listening partner relationship offers us. I want to make a suggestion that if you have someone who is an anchor in your life right now, or a potential anchor, ask them if they would like to be your listening partner, beginning now and especially for part 2 of this book. Holding space for each other as you each begin to do some inner work can provide a safe container for going deep into the territory of your wounds. If you don't have someone in mind, maybe this is just a seed being planted so that when the right person appears, you will find the courage to ask them to join you. None of us can just go to the supermarket and buy anchors, but we can begin to get a sense of what we need and want.

Awakening the bodily feeling of being with the anchors of our earlier lives can also help us recognize when someone is bringing that kind of safety to us now. Maybe we already have such people but haven't been thinking about our relationships that way. None of them will be perfect, but perhaps some have a natural tendency to listen deeply and offer observations with humility and generosity. We can also ask friends who have a penchant for fixing us if they would like to try to do it differently. If we are carrying a lot of early wounding, we might begin the search to find a therapist with a strong capacity for being truly and safely present. Just opening our hearts and minds to the possibility of being joined in this beauti-fully safe way is the beginning.

The Practice of Listening Deeply

Once we have someone who is willing to take this leap into intimacy with us, we can begin practicing with the expectation that this is a long-term process with all kinds of ups and downs, detours, celebrations, and dedication to continuing no matter what arises. We get to do it wrong a hundred times, become tender toward our own and each other's humanity, and make heartfelt repairs. Out of all this comes a growing capacity for holding each other. The whole world will benefit from more of that.

Here's a little helpful guidance on speaking and listening deeply, just to get you started. Each couple's process will be unique, and each time the two of you share, new dimensions will reveal themselves. Even if you don't have a listening partner yet, this way of listening can be helpful in all relationships.

1. It's always a good idea to check in with your listening partner or companion to see if they have the bandwidth to listen at this moment. You might say something like, "I have something to share and I'm wondering if you feel like you could receive it right now." Then pause for your partner to respond.

It's important that the two of you have agreed in advance that "this isn't the best time for me, can we talk later?" is an okay answer, especially when it's followed by an agreement to meet again later. This said, if your partner's answer to your request is no, some old abandonment pain may come up. Your listening partner may also feel guilty saying no. Just noticing together what comes up for you both when you have these moments when one person has to take a rain check on connecting can be so helpful. Honesty is essential to safety and also sometimes very challenging because perhaps our honesty has not always been well received in the past.

2. If the answer is yes, you can take a couple of deeper breaths, centering yourself in your body. If you are the listener, you can also take a couple of breaths to quiet and open yourself to receiving. The one sharing can offer a few sentences about what is coming up. When we are upset, we sometimes have a tendency to speak quickly and share everything at once. Slowing down helps both speaker and listener to connect with what is being said and felt.

3. While the speaker is sharing, the listener can notice if they are able to stay with just listening. Our minds

often naturally begin to comment on what is being said, sometimes even preparing what we are going to say in response even before the speaker is finished talking. When this happens, just notice it and let as much of the need to respond go as you can, without judgment. It's just part of being human. Come back to simply listening and holding space for your listening partner when you can.

4. When the speaker pauses, the listener can ask the speaker if they would like a reflection. If the answer is yes, you might say something like, "What I hear you saying is . . ." As best you can, capture the felt sense and meaning of what you heard. This may include reflecting the words themselves. However, repeating the exact words is often the least important part of the reflection. If only the words are reflected, the exchange may feel mechanical and unsatisfying to both people. Choosing words that reflect your own understanding of what your partner said coupled with your presence is what matters most.

5. You can finish your reflection with something like, "Does that feel like I got that right?" If not, the speaker shares what felt missed or misunderstood.

This isn't about perfect accuracy, but about deepening the connection between the two of you so that the speaker feels embraced and understood at the same time. It may take several tries to get there.

6. When it feels like the speaker may be settling and finishing, the listener can ask, "Is there anything more?" Then just pause while the listener senses if anything else is coming up.

7. Check in with your bodies to see what may have changed during this conversation. When we feel truly heard, there are often changes in our bodies as our inner world signals it has felt received. There may be a release of tension in the belly, chest, and muscles; a softening in the throat and other places; tears, smiles, or laughter. The listener may also notice something changing as they are touched by what is being shared. They might feel warm and tender or perhaps stirred up by what was communicated. Once the speaker is heard, they will often feel very receptive to hearing what happened for their partner.

8. It's fine to stop right here, and as listening partners, you may also want to share what the process was

like for each of you. The listener might tell their partner about moments when they felt like fixing them or when their mind was preparing an answer. The speaker might share the fear or ease in sharing deeply. This kind of open and humble and deeply human sharing builds safety and trust, paving the way for even deeper sharing over time.

As true safety settles in with the arrival of our anchors and listening partners, our natural response is to become more vulnerable. Our system is always leaning toward healing and will begin to open once the needed support is in place. The greater the trust, the more our inner world responds by making its wounds available for healing. It is as if our entire system knows that we are not meant to do this work alone, that true healing occurs in partnership with others.

True healing occurs in partnership with others.

The key is to listen, *as best you can*. The heart of our work is to develop the capacity to be present without judgment or agenda, with open ears, eyes, heart, and mind. Two things tend to happen when we fail to simply listen. One is that we begin to prepare our response while the other person is still speaking. At that point, any connection is lost. Often it just happens without our intention at all. In this culture, it has become as natural as breathing. We may hope that the other person doesn't notice, but they do, even if they aren't conscious of it. At the subtle level of their autonomic nervous system, they will feel shut out. At the moment we leave them for our own thoughts, the connection is temporarily broken for both of us. We are each alone.

The other thing that often happens when we stop truly listening is we notice an intense need to offer advice, to fix the situation. As we become more aware, we might discover that our heart rate has increased and that we are feeling some level of fear right as this urge to take control and fix things begins to overwhelm us. Even if we manage to resist the impulse to fix, the energy between us will shift in a way that, again, we may both begin to feel alone.

Both of the above happen to everyone, so the next important thing is to be able to acknowledge when it is happening with as little judgment as possible. One of the most valuable aspects of a listening partnership is cultivating enough trust to be able to speak about our struggle to listen without feeling ashamed about it. We are just human beings, growing up in a left-hemisphere-dominant culture that is much more comfortable fixing things than receiving each other with a quiet mind and open heart. Every time we are able to offer this kind of gentle, receptive environment for one another, we are building new neural circuitry that will make it more familiar and more natural the next time. What we are giving one another is the experience of *co-regulation*, a refuge of safety where we can do the delicate work of healing old wounds.

Rachel Naomi Remen, physician, author, and mystic, says this about listening:

Listening is the oldest and perhaps the most powerful tool of healing. It is often through the quality of our listening and not the wisdom of our words that we are able to effect the most profound changes in the people around us. When we listen, we offer with our attention an opportunity for wholeness. Our listening creates sanctuary for the homeless parts within the other person. That which has been denied, unloved, devalued by themselves and by others. That which is hidden. In this culture, the soul and the heart too often go homeless. Listening creates a holy silence. When you listen generously to people, they can hear truth in themselves, often for the first time. And in the silence of listening, you can know yourself in everyone. Eventually, you may be able to hear, in everyone and beyond everyone, the unseen singing softly to itself and to you.

When we have the good fortune to have people in our lives who are able to truly listen to us, we find ourselves able to deepen in such unexpected ways. Your chosen listening partner, or even two or three, will be dedicated to making the journey with you. Perhaps you will even choose to read and reflect on this book together. A theme we will return to again and again is that the healing process happens in the warm embrace of others. Finding your anchors and listening partners is a crucial first step in the journey.

ONE LAST (AND POSSIBLY UNEXPECTED) ANCHOR

Knowledge can be an important anchor as well. In moments when I felt most unsure of how I might emerge out of the pain of losing the relationship I described in chapter 1, surprisingly it was science that kept me going. Understanding how our brains work through studying relational neuroscience can help us put the pieces together when we feel most alone. It gives us the scientific evidence that we do in fact need each other—that it isn't actually best to be self-sufficient, self-regulating, and approaching life as a solo mission. Needing others is not a weakness we must overcome. Relational neuroscience teaches us that this is contrary to our nature. We are meant to be in connection with one another throughout our lives. With this knowledge, we can reorient ourselves to a different way of living. With this new understanding, maybe we've learned just enough to gain some clear-sighted awareness of the importance of the true psychological safety that is found within each other. Maybe we can see ourselves with a little more compassion, too.

One of my mentors-at-a-distance, Iain McGilchrist, seminal scholar of the two hemispheres of the brain, talks about the importance of integrating the right hemisphere (which gives us the emotional capacity for being present with one another) with the left hemisphere (which holds the intellectual understanding of how we humans get hurt and heal). When relationship and knowledge work together, we can find a balance between the often painful and activating work of touching our attachment wounds and the ability to stand slightly back from the process to know that we're on the right path.

THE POWER OF "HOLDING HANDS" IN HARD TIMES

Researcher James Coan and his colleagues explore the effects of being in trustworthy connection with others. Their work, which they call Social Baseline Theory, reveals that we are better able to move through challenges—and even thrive despite them—when we feel held in the warmth and care of others. In one of their studies, participants are put in a scanner and receive a mild electric shock. Other participants are put in the same scanner and also given a mild electric shock, but they are able to hold hands with someone close to them through the experience. When asked about the degree of pain they felt, the subjects who were able to hold hands with a person dear to them felt less pain than those who had to go it alone. The study revealed the power of being with people who we have a bond with through pain or difficulty. This is a remarkable discovery. Without doing anything except being present, we make life easier for each other. This is true for physically painful experiences, but also for any task that feels difficult. Metaphorically or physically holding hands calms the amygdala (the part of our brain that is involved in sensing safety and danger) so that our system settles. All of our fears about being alone are valid. Isolation is painful. Being in close proximity to people who offer us safety is the glue that can help us through life's challenges.

Often when you leave a relationship like the one I described in chapter 1, even though the connection doesn't feel fundamentally safe, it still provides some sense of protection against the terror of being isolated and alone. In the beginning, when I was first with this partner, I would run into his arms whenever I needed to feel safe, and for the first couple of years of our relationship, I really did feel safe. And even as we grew more and more distant and he moved further and further away from me, I kept running to him to try and get back into connection. However, as I progressed further along in my own healing journey, I realized that the power to feel supported could not lie in the hands of just one person but rather in the collective strength of my anchors. Transitioning from relying on my emotionally unavailable partner—hoping he would fix me and then being upset when the pain remained—to drawing on the strength of trusted friends and professionals marked a significant turn in my journey toward inner security and deeper relationships. It was far from easy, because being with people I could trust with my tenderness and my fear was extremely challenging. It meant that I had to acknowledge my pain. But they remained steadfast, even when I was at my most vulnerable points. Gradually, what I learned was that my anchors had the power to help me feel held and supported in my own experience—no matter how painful it was.

At first, I depended on them a lot, calling them daily and learning to trust that they were there for me. I would drive to my friend Julia's house just to see her face, leave my friend Melissa a video message to stay in contact, see my therapist, and even reach out to her on some of my harder days. What I found was that everyone responded to me as best they could. People showed up and made repairs when something disturbed our connection. Their consistent presence in my life led me to trust more and more that I could lean on them, and in time I was able to internalize their care to the point that when they were physically absent, I didn't feel abandoned.

Over time, as more healing took place, I began to feel these connections *inside* me. I started to experience waves of gratitude because I could feel certain people *with* me when I was alone. This is the very experience that develops in the first two years as babies experience a secure attachment with their parents. It is wonderful that, as adults, we can receive what was missed when we were small. We call this new experience that is emerging inside *earned security*. And I have to be honest, in my experience it did feel very much earned because I was so used to running to romantic partners in an attempt to drown my pain. I didn't know what it meant to have others to simply be *with me* in my pain—to hold and make space for it. It was slow and difficult work, but as I gradually allowed myself to be vulnerable with my anchors, the feelings of safety I felt were so much deeper and richer than anything I had experienced before. I now believe that, when we take people in, an invisible thread begins to develop between us, and the deeper the connection becomes, the more our feelings of being safe and secure in the world can grow.

What unfolded was an evolution from externally needing and seeking security to cultivating an *internal sanctuary* of genuine support and connection. This journey, while deeply personal, echoes the universal potential for healing through relational bonds. I'd like you to imagine me holding your hand—or perhaps being in the room with you—while you begin building on any past experiences where you felt held and cared for. As you move through these pages, my biggest wish for you is that these principles resonate with you, nurturing a profound feeling of support that you can sense within, both physically and emotionally. May these messages enable you to develop an understanding that you, too, can experience the effects of shared healing and discover a newfound strength in your inner and outer worlds.

CHAPTER 3

WELCOMING YOUR INNER PROTECTORS

For many years of my life, I was a "Yes" girl. I took great pride in my ability to be there for anyone who needed me, even at the drop of a hat. As a result, I took on way more than I could possibly handle. My schedule was always packed. I didn't realize it then, but my need to always be on the move was an attempt to avoid my inner pain and suffering. It was the only way I knew how to feel "safe"—even if the safety wasn't real. Inevitably, the void I felt inside would catch up with me and I'd realize that I actually had no safe place to turn. When this happened, I'd quickly go back to working like a little machine.

As adults, our attachment experiences from childhood are always playing in the background. If these experiences were largely "insecure," we tend to lead our lives more on either the anxious or avoidant end of the spectrum. While on the surface we may appear quite functional, successful even, on the inside we are operating according to the adaptations we developed when we were very young in order to survive.

During these years when I said yes to most everything anyone asked or expected of me, everyone knew me as "successful"—and I was always busy proving it. However, on the rare occasions that I would slow down a little, a nearly disabling amount of anxiety and discomfort would reverberate throughout my being. My body was screaming at me, a desperate plea for attention that I ignored for the sake of survival. This led me to experience moments of complete disconnection from my body. My head felt like it was floating, detached from the rest of me. It was as if I was observing my life rather than living it.

Now I realize that my way of being during these years is what happens when we retreat into the left-hemisphere way of perceiving the world, which provides us with a form of protection from our own suffering by disconnecting us from our bodies. The left hemisphere of our brain focuses us on tasks rather than relationships. This razor-sharp focus serves us well when we need to solve a complicated math problem or navigate a practical decision at work, but it does so at the expense of our ability to register the emotional dimensions of our experience. Then again, this can be a relief when what we are feeling in our body is fear, pain, or aloneness. In these moments, staying with our left hemisphere can allow us to disconnect from these emotions, giving us a temporary shelter when we don't yet have the supportive people we need to tolerate the accumulated trauma.

Not everyone adapts by becoming a human *doing* rather than a human *being*, although our culture certainly rewards that method of staying away from pain. Others may collapse into hopelessness or turn to addictive substances in an attempt to numb themselves or fill up the empty spaces with warm feelings, even if it's only a temporary fix. There are any number of ways we may find to shut down and make our lives smaller. We each do it in the best way we know how.

It's no surprise that around this time, I landed in the emergency room because I thought I was having a heart attack. My body was tight with unbearable tension, and any small movements would cause painful sensations in my chest. This strange, sharp pain kept shooting out from my rib cage and I feared the worst. The doctor told me I had something called "Devil's Grip." I wasn't having a heart attack, but the stress and inflammation in my body were reaching such a level that it was impossible to not notice the sensations. My body, in its wisdom, was making its pain known before irreparable harm was done. Oscillating between pain and numbness, I booked massage after massage in hopes of feeling a moment of relief. I spent endless hours in the bathtub, took medication to sleep, and revved myself up to stay busy all day. If I paused to take a vacation, I would feel even worse because I had taken away my protective busyness.

As I look back, I realize that I was primarily driven by a hustle culture that teaches us that being successful, pretty, popular, and "perfect" is the pathway to happiness. The looming fear of failing as a stepmother coupled with my partner's plea to reduce my workload was eating away at me, so I knew I needed to make some changes.

Bonnie Badenoch's book *The Heart of Trauma* came into my hands at just the moment when I needed it most. It's the way she tells the story of how we are hurt and how we heal that touched me most. In a compassionate voice, she explains how our attachment experiences live on inside us. We wisely learn how to protect ourselves from the ongoing pain, but these wounds continue to guide how we live in the world. She described a pathway of healing based on safe relationships rather than techniques, and that touched something deep inside me. I sensed this was what I wanted and needed.

I reached out to Bonnie and she ultimately led me to a therapist, Jo, who could go deeply with me. As I traveled further and further down the path of healing, I entrusted my company's responsibilities to capable hands, relinquishing my grip on control. It was time to deal with what my body had been holding for years. Bit by bit, I began to decelerate and be with what needed to come up. Hello, grief. I was beginning to get in touch with the pain surrounding my attachment wounds, discovering what I had missed and what I needed to grieve from my childhood. In this relationship, I felt the deep sense of safety I needed to experience in order to heal.

I didn't just arrive here overnight, though. I had been leading life from my control-addicted left hemisphere for a long time. It was my protective way of being and it was not possible, or even wise, to just walk away from it. Jo and I moved slowly as I learned to listen to the channel of information that was coming up from my body to my brain's right hemisphere—which is where we store trauma, and also where we heal it. I had to learn to be with my attachment wounds in a new way. A key to doing this was to bring them to people whom I could trust and who could offer me the safe haven I needed.

As we begin to explore the origins of our attachment wounds together, we will also start to understand what protections we have needed to survive the pain and avoid feeling these deep wounds that we store in our bodies. These core wounds, tucked protectively away in our subconscious, prompt us to go to great lengths to avoid drowning in them, and for good reason. Without the right support and understanding, they can be overwhelmingly scary and painful. But the more we avoid them, the more drawn we are to situations that reenact them in our daily lives.

Meanwhile, cultural norms also do their work of keeping us stuck in place. We live in a world that enforces the viewpoint that there is strength in standing alone—an idea that is counterproductive to what we truly need to heal old wounds and to stay healthy in our lives. As we begin to understand how our culture idealizes the independence and self-reliance championed by our left hemisphere (which focuses on the sense of "I," on tasks and performance, on being in control) over what the right hemisphere brings to the table (the sense of "we," the capacity for warm relationships, and also the truth of what we feel emotionally and physically), we can begin to gain some compassion for why healing attachment wounds is so hard and counterintuitive. This restless pursuit of personal pleasure, success, and survival, heavily aided by technology and our ever-increasing screen time, not only distances us from the essential work of healing our attachment wounds but also ensnares us in chronic fear states of sympathetic arousal (where our bodies are perpetually ready to fight or flee) and dissociated states (where we feel numb or detached from our physical selves). These conditions insulate us from the lived, felt experience of our bodies, hindering our deep desire and need for meaning and genuine, heartfelt connection, and pushing us more into the territory of isolation and loneliness. Psychologist Barbara Fredrickson's research tells us that about 75 percent of us in the developed world are living like this now, cut off from meaningful connection with one another in ways that injure our physical as well as emotional health. These cycles of detachment make the journey back to ourselves and each other all the more arduous. Healing begins with understanding that what is actually needed to heal is *safe people and safe environments*.

This raises an important question. How did we get here?

TRACING THE ROOTS OF OUR DISCONNECTION

At least ten thousand years ago, those of us in the Western world began to turn away from a culture based on "we" to a culture based on "I." Some historians say that the move from hunting and gathering to farming was the turning point, and others suggest different cultural shifts. Regardless of the exact cause and timing, it is clear that as we left communal life for individual life, we became afraid.

The moment I experience myself as having something I can call mine, the possibility that it will be taken away comes alive. I must protect it, and if possible, get more of it so I will feel secure. The problem is that this kind of material security isn't at all the same as interpersonal safety because the danger of loss will always loom in the background. Under these circumstances, competition, hierarchy, and many other means of self-protection flourish at the expense of the safety that comes from community and connection.

How do our brains help us adapt under these conditions? The brain in our skull has two hemispheres. The illuminating research of psychiatrist Iain McGilchrist, who has written extensively about these two hemispheres, tells us that it is like having two people in our brains who see and experience the world very differently. When we are seeing and relating from the perspective of the right hemisphere, we are open to the goodness of warm, meaningful relationships. But for this to happen, we have to feel safe. Through Stephen Porges's and Iain McGilchrist's research, we understand that fear brings our left hemisphere forward because that helps us take control of whatever feels threatening. Our left hemisphere is good at making judgments about what is right or wrong. It focuses us on the task at hand so we can address the danger. When we're scared, this is adaptive. But in this state, our system can't find safety through connection in any consistent way. With so many centuries of being afraid, our culture is drenched in left-hemisphere values.

So many of my clients come into my office telling me that they need therapy in order to take control of their lives. I remember one client in particular. In our first meeting, Archie shared that she hadn't gotten the promotion she had earned and expected. "I'm lying in bed shaking every night, because how can I be worth anything to anyone when I can't even get ahead at work?" As we sat with these feelings of failure, she began to see images of her father's disapproving face. "He would be so ashamed of me," she said, with her head down, her shoulders pulled in tightly. He had passed away ten years ago, but he was definitely with us in this room. It was clear that the only way he knew how to love his daughter was by trying to shame her into being what he believed the culture required of her—a success.

For us now as we explore more and more deeply what protections we humans default to in order to escape our fears and to feel some semblance of safety, the most important thing to understand about left-hemisphere dominance is that it can lead us to lose all sense of being in relationship with others. Everything and everyone become tools in our elusive quest for safety. For example, when our left hemispheres are dominant, we focus on what people can do for us rather than feeling connected to them with our hearts. We can't help it. It's just the way the left hemisphere sees and manages the world when it is cut off from the relational right hemisphere.

We can get a taste of how we experience these two hemispheres if we consider how we relate to our precious bodies. When we come from the perspective of the left, we boss our bodies around. We demand that they do many reps at the gym, wear certain kinds of clothes that display body shapes that are approved by the current cultural standards. Failure in any of these areas can make us miserable. All sense of individuality is lost in a sea of what the culture considers the right way for all of us to be. If we show up from the right hemisphere, the world begins to feel very different. We begin to get into relationship with our bodies. We begin to listen to what our bodies need at any given moment. That is the key—we listen. We get into a conversation. We enjoy that we are individuals and that our needs change from moment to moment. There is gentleness and respect.

As Archie and I began to explore her inner world more deeply, we took note of the sensations that were showing up in her body. First, her inner father arrived to let her know what he expected of her. Her body began to share its story of shame through her lowered head and shoulders. Before too long, her deeper inner world began to let us know how utterly alone she had felt all her life. Her body felt cold, with a deep pit of emptiness in her belly. She shivered. With tenderness, we stayed with the sensations until they began to settle and she noticed the beginning of a warm feeling in her chest. Reflecting on her teen years, she told me, "I had quite a few friends in high school. At least it looked like I did. But now I wonder if that was really true at all. I just ached with loneliness so much of the time, even back then."

The saddest part of left dominance is that, while it may help us deal with our fear, it also leaves us feeling alone—even in the midst of a crowd, even when we have an active social life, and often even when we are in an intimate partnership. Since meaning and fulfillment depend on safety and connection, in addition to whatever scared us into our left hemisphere in the first place, we now have the pain and fear that being alone brings us. This is a difficult pattern to change without safe companions, which is part of why we read about the crisis of loneliness in the news so often these days.

However, embedded deep within each of us, safety and connection are still biological imperatives, always encouraging us in the direction of seeking warm relationships.

When we have had parents who have also been engulfed in this culture that tells us we should be successful little machines, that being safe means acquiring status, money, and achievements, we absorb this way of being as a means of staying connected with them. When our parents, like Archie's, are influencing us this way, it's because they truly believe this will make us happy. It is a form of love that injures us.

As we learn to slow down and allow the right hemisphere to take the lead, gradually we can invite people who feel safe to hold space for us in our suffering. Yet allowing others into our pain can be daunting because our inclination is to avoid our suffering at all costs. After all, we have developed reliable patterns of behavior and relating to protect ourselves in order to function at all in the world.

You know the saying that pain gets passed down from generation to generation, demanding to be felt? Well, many of us grew up in homes where avoidance as a means of surviving is intergenerational. We are fortunate to live in a time when getting help is much more encouraged. The fact that there are now ads on television and the internet featuring celebrities of all sorts sending the message that "It's okay to ask for help" is a true blessing. My parents certainly had no easily available resources. It takes a tremendous amount of courage, the right support, and safe environments for us to slow down and begin to heal these intergenerational wounds.

MEETING OUR PROTECTORS

Often, the very first step toward healing, once we have our anchoring people in place, is to meet and learn to value those parts of ourselves that have brilliantly provided protection from the intolerable pain and fear we have felt inside. This is where Archie and I began—appreciating that her drive toward success and her enormous investment in the world of work were doing what they could to keep her safe from the emptiness within. Now it was time for her to meet her inner Protectors.

Our protectors are actually our system's attempt to shield us from emotional pain and uncertainty. Many of them, including avoidance and those critical internal voices in our heads telling us to move quickly and do what society or family expects of us, operate out of our left hemisphere. These protectors urge us to move fast toward the top of the food chain, or to find temporary comfort in activities like overeating, excessive shopping, or overindulging in work. These inner protectors are brilliant adaptations to safeguard us from our underlying pain. They have been our companions throughout our struggles, stepping in to fill the void left by unmet needs and unhealed wounds. Although we might initially resist or even dislike our protectors, recognizing them as valuable allies in our journey through adversity marks a meaningful internal transformation.

Instead of wanting to make them go away, Archie and I began

to say to them, "Everyone is welcome here. Tell me your story. What would have happened to me without you? What kind of pain and fear are you protecting me from feeling?" By recognizing these parts of herself as allies, we began to reduce the inner battle to more manageable proportions. These parts of herself were also the gatekeepers of her deeper inner world, so befriending them meant the source of her upset was going to become more available to us.

Welcoming our protectors because we experience them as necessary adaptations, rather than hindrances to getting better, is crucial to our healing. We all have them even if we are not aware of them or precisely what they are protecting. The critical voices many of us wrestle with, often reflections of societal pressures or echoing the demands of a critical parent, serve as necessary guardrails, trying to protect us from failure in our pursuit of unattainable perfection. The answer to Archie's question about who the shaming voices inside her were protecting is the child who was judged and prodded by a father scared of the consequences for his beloved daughter failing at anything. As we softened toward her protectors, they brought this child forward for us to receive her without judgment and comfort her with full hearts. We were even able to sense that this inner father was full of love for her, even though his disapproving looks and words had humiliated her so painfully.

As these wounded parts of ourselves begin healing, our protectors will no longer be needed in the same way. For Archie, this meant that compassion for herself and her father began to gradually replace the waves of shame she had been enduring every day. Slowly, with many inner visits, she and her inner father found a good measure of reconciliation and peace.

A Practice for Identifying and Embracing Our Protectors

Once we begin to find our anchors, the most helpful place for us to begin our healing process together is to get to know our protectors. If you have found a listening partner, you will give each other the support you need to go more deeply into this process. Slowing down together is the first step. Embracing all the responses each of you has to these parts of yourselves is so important. Your journal can also be your partner as you invite your protectors to come into your awareness. Journaling isn't always in words, either. I have found that sometimes my protectors have colors and even images that let me deepen into the felt sense of how they are with me. My tendency to drift away into dissociation has a gray quality and looks like fog. My familiar go-to of over-working looks like orange tangled string. Some combination of words and drawing has been most helpful for me.

It's possible that your first inner reaction will be to push some of these protectors away, letting them know how much you don't like them. This is a protection, too! So we can begin to welcome that impulse as well.

As you stay with it, this practice will help you deepen your understanding—and acceptance—of your inner protectors, sensing that they are vital members of your pain avoidance team. To provide a few examples, your well-developed army might include distraction, chocolate, books, alcohol, saying yes when you want to say no, judging others, compulsive attention to social media, playing computer games, and being busy, busy, busy. Anything that you do compulsively in response to a sense of something uncomfortable emerging. Engaging with this process allows us to explore the often-unconscious protections we deploy, each of us in our own uniquely adaptive way.

Let's begin.

Step 1: Reflection and Recognition

Start by finding a quiet, comfortable space where you and your journal or you and your partner can reflect without interruption. If you are with your listening partner, decide who will do the exploration first, with the other as the nonjudgmental listener and support. If it feels comfortable, take a few deep breaths to center yourself. Invite yourself to reflect on a recent moment when you felt overwhelmed or distressed. See if you can notice what protective response stepped in. Was it some form of denial, avoiding the reality of the situation? Repression, pushing away unwanted thoughts? Or perhaps intellectualization, diving into the analytical to avoid emotional pain and gain some sense of control? Or did you just get very busy? Find some ice cream or start mindlessly scrolling through social media to get relief? Maybe you poured yourself a glass of wine, cracked open a beer, or took another hit off your vape? Some of us may notice that when shame wells up in us, we have a strong impulse to put on our running clothes and do enough laps around the block to exhaust ourselves—anything to stop our bodies from collapsing into our shame. Our protectors are as individual as our fingerprints. And sometimes it takes several of them to manage our pain or fear.

Step 2: Sharing Your Experience

Even if you haven't found a permanent listening partner yet, it may be that you have an anchoring person with whom you could share what you are noticing. When the two of you hold these parts, a different quality of comfort and compassion becomes available. It is more than one plus one because of the way we share nervous systems. If it is hard for you to welcome this part, perhaps your person can do that for you. When we are tenderly heard and received, our ability to welcome even challenging protectors broadens and deepens in often surprising ways.

Step 3: Mapping Your Protectors

On a piece of paper, draw a simple chart or list. Name each protector you've identified, and next to it, write down the specific feelings that come up in your body when this part of you is near. Then see if you can begin to sense the feelings and memories it's trying to safeguard you from, as best you can tell. Often, it is more than one feeling or experience, and sometimes what is being protected isn't quite clear. However, this act of mapping is a powerful acknowledgment of your protectors' presence and purpose. If you keep some markers or crayons nearby, you may find that each protector has their own color or wants you to draw an image. Moving into color and drawing can often help to make the felt sense of the protector more vivid as you invite the right-hemisphere experience. It may turn out that each protector needs their own page!

Step 4: Engaging in Dialogue

Ask yourself which protector would like to come forward. This part of you is more like a person than a thing, and with practice you'll find that you can have a conversation with them.

- It can be very helpful to begin with a gesture of welcome if that feels natural to you. "Thank you for coming" or "Hi there, glad you're here." If these don't feel true, begin with what is most natural for you. If a protector arrives who alarms you in some way, be honest about that. This conversation can begin anywhere.

- After a sense of relationship is established, you might ask, "Who or what are you trying to protect me from?" You may need to ask more than once because you are asking not so much to get concrete information as to gently allow your inner world the possibility of moving closer to the parts inside of you who are so fiercely being guarded by your protectors. In these moments, you will experience a right-hemisphere process of opening to connection rather than a left-hemisphere process of accessing pieces of information to build "knowledge."

Rather than requiring an answer, the dialogue you are having with your inner world is more like dropping a question into your right hemisphere and just waiting to see what happens. At first, little may happen, as your protectors are quite used to guiding your behaviors and responses to the world unnoticed. If you persist with your warm curiosity, an answer might come in the form of an image or memory or a felt sense in your body rather than a clear knowing. Going slow and listening is the key, recognizing this dialogue as an important step toward entering your inner world.

Step 5: Expressing Gratitude

Take a moment to express your gratitude toward each protector for their role in shielding you from intolerable pain and fear, even if the methods might not always seem helpful. As your understanding of the wisdom of these parts of you grows, you will develop greater compassion for the inner parts of yourself that need healing.

Step 6: Envisioning a Partnership

It may be helpful to visualize a future where these protectors are acknowledged and don't need to work so hard because your attachment wounds are gradually healing. What might that look like for you? How might this protector become an ally? Many of us may discover, as I did, that when our incessant drive for success isn't our only means for defining our worth, we can shift all of our tremendous ability to focus and work hard into enriching all the areas of our lives that need attention (not just our jobs!).

Step 7: Committing to Healing

With your listening partner or in your journal, acknowledge that while these protectors have played a crucial role in your survival, you are both now on a path to healing that involves facing your pain with courage and support. Commit to gently uncovering the feelings and experiences these protectors are guarding.

Making a commitment to this practice of acknowledging protectors regularly sends a message to our inner world that we are fully engaged in healing. There is really no end to the variety and creativity of our protectors, so there will always be something new to discover when we do this. As we continue on this journey, we allow ourselves to move toward a life filled with more genuine connections—both internally and externally—along with increasing inner peace and resilience. Soon you'll find that the more safe people and supportive environments you connect with, the more in tune you will become with the protectors living inside you. This was the case with Dan, a client who embarked on a journey to heal his core wounds through an online course I facilitated.

SAFETY IS THE TREATMENT

Dan was a member of a closed group of ten clients I met with virtually for two hours a week for eight weeks. At the group's first meeting, I started with the question, "What comes up in your body when you hear the word 'codependency'?" A few of the group members said they felt something in their chest or their belly, but Dan shared that he could not feel anything in his body. He told us that the only thing he felt aware of was frantically searching his mind for the right answer. Everyone listened respectfully and then moved on. I felt warmth in my chest as he shared his struggle, tenderly curious about what kind of pain was requiring him to protect himself with such a complete cutoff from his sensations.

In the first couple of sessions, group members share something about their history and current circumstances as a way of getting to know each other and establishing a sense of safety. Dan told us his parents were immigrants who had struggled to make ends meet. In his home growing up, he had little room for anything but focusing on the tasks necessary to survive. He and his siblings were consumed by the intensity of accomplishing the tasks of daily life. He shared all of this in a flat manner and without any emotion. One of the group members asked him if he felt loved by his parents when he was growing up. He paused a long time and, with a puzzled look on his face, said simply, "I suppose so."

The members also shared what brought them to this group. Several of them talked about becoming aware that they had experienced trauma or attachment wounds in their lives and wanting to heal. Dan told us he was there because his wife was concerned that he was depressed. She'd told him that she felt lonely because there wasn't much emotional connection between them. He admitted that he was unable to even find joy with his children. Dan told us that he had been confused by what his wife had said, but sitting there with us was making him realize that he did feel numb and detached a lot of the time.

By the third week, Dan was sharing his concern that nothing was going to change for him. His openness about that seemed to shift something for the whole group. In a tender way, everyone seemed to come to his side, reassuring him that they could be with him exactly as he was. We had been exploring protectors, and one of the women said to Dan, "I believe that being numb is the only way you can protect yourself from how alone and lost you have always been. You've seen me. Sometimes all I can do is get really mad to protect myself." I saw his hand go to his belly for a moment, but I didn't want to ask him what was happening out of concern for scaring the feeling away. Instead, the whole group, collectively, took him in just as he was. We sat with his sensations of feeling detached, numb, and separated from his body. The words he found to describe this were "walled off." With this awareness of a sensation, he was giving his protector a name. I celebrated silently inside. Something was happening in this safe and caring space.

Dan showed up week after week, and the group supported him (and one another), no matter what. Together we had created a safe container for all of their sensations and early memories to be held. Sometimes, vulnerable experiences from early childhood paid a visit. Other times protectors took the lead, trying to keep pain or sadness at bay. In this sanctuary that welcomed every experience, Dan began to see and feel the presence of a little boy with sad eyes, working very hard to be part of this family in the only way he could. The ultimate testament to the meaning of this group for him came on the last day we met. At the end of that group, he asked me for the name of a therapist who would be present for him in the same way.

One of the things Dan shared in our last meeting was his sense that he had no control over this process. He knew—and could share—that it was the presence of this group and the power of the support that had helped him recognize his protectors, and was now letting his body and heart begin to awaken to the truth of his early experiences. In a very real and embodied way, he was starting to feel both the love that his parents had for their children and the daily stress that kept them focused solely on survival.

Acknowledging our wounds can be a painful experience, but it is important to remember that because our brains are remarkably flexible throughout life and profoundly receptive to being truly seen in relationship, our wounds are not a life sentence. The nonjudgmental presence and safety of others is often enough to begin the healing process. When one or more of these trusted supporters arrive and hold us safely in their arms, a vast healing wisdom that already resides within us is unleashed.

But how exactly does this healing occur? When we are able to truly be there for one another, our nervous systems engage in what is referred to as *co-regulation*. As Dan was embraced by the members of our group, our autonomic nervous systems came together to provide a net of safety that allowed Dan's painful and fearful experiences to emerge. Co-regulation can happen between two or more people.

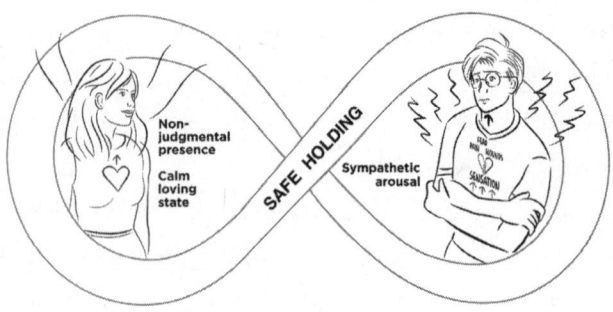

When we are activated or in a shutdown state, it is really hard to connect. However, when someone holds space for us in this calmer state of safety, it is contagious. In a real way, we become one nervous system. That kind of holding eventually allows for painful early memories that are often connected to our attachment wounds to come to the surface and receive what they need to integrate.

The magic in having space held is that the safer you feel in the presence of another person, the more your body's inherent wisdom allows for memories to start to surface. The more we can be with what is happening inside us, and allow another to help hold space for us, the less we will need the behaviors and protections we've been relying on to avoid our pain. Now healing can begin. Shortly after the group ended, I received a call from Dan's wife. She said he was playing in the backyard with their three kids, laughing and enjoying himself in a way she hadn't seen in years. What joy that gave me!

Our wounds are not a life sentence.

For whatever reason and with no blame assigned, there is a good chance many of us didn't get enough of this kind of presence and holding when we were small. Perhaps our parents were struggling to get ahead in life or had some fears that overwhelmed their ability to really be with us in this way consistently. When our parents and parents' parents have been just surviving in the world, we have likely been absorbing a lot of their wounds. That has meant our systems wisely and adaptively tucked away these memories of pain and fear in our bellies, hearts, muscles, and more, just waiting for the right support to come forward so they can receive what they need and be healed.

CREATING SPACE FOR VULNERABILITY

When our bodies begin to relax into the true safety and presence of another, we are invited into the healing intimacy we crave. But we may also encounter a paradox that can give us pause. We can ask ourselves, "Is it really okay now to let my guard down?" Listening to the synonyms for vulnerability—powerless, unguarded, delicate, at the mercy of, unprotected, weak—can illuminate the heart of this paradox. Allow yourself to let all of the mixed feelings in your body emerge. Maybe sensations of feeling exposed or at someone's mercy are rising to the surface. Or perhaps you find yourself recalling in your body moments when you felt similarly fragile and were met by the warm, safe embrace of a friend. All of this is part of the experience. Take them in as they arrive, allowing yourself to face the ambiguity of dancing between protection and vulnerability in these early stages of your healing journey.

At the beginning of my therapy, I was fairly guarded, often taking refuge in my rational left hemisphere. I had a legitimate need to understand the process, a protective need to not get too vulnerable too soon, and underneath it all, an aching need to be comforted in the heartbreak I was feeling. As my therapeutic relationship with Jo deepened, memories of early loss began to surface on their own, as images and as feelings in my body. At the same time, my system was opening to receive the attentive care Jo was offering. I was both in great pain and healing. These are the twin experiences of vulnerability.

In her groundbreaking work, Brené Brown shares that vulnerability is not a sign of weakness, but rather the birthplace of courage, creativity, and connection. She argues that by embracing our vulnerability, we open ourselves up to the possibility of experiencing love, belonging, and deep fulfilling connection. All of this is true.

However, this path is not without its challenges. It involves acknowledging our imperfections, fears, and shortcomings. Shame, the feeling that something is wrong with me, frequently accompanies attachment wounds. When we are small, our parents' reflection of who we are is everything. If, in their pain, they look at us as a problem, a disappointment, a burden, then we may feel unwanted or ugly or wrong for existing. The resulting shame keeps us small and turned away from life or leads us to inflate ourselves and demand attention from wounded others. Committing to this healing path means we will once again feel the depths of rejection, but within the embrace of the receptive care of another.

One of the gifts of vulnerability is that it has the power to create a sense of belonging and community. When we share our vulnerabilities, it creates a ripple effect that encourages others to do the same. This nurtures a culture of acceptance, empathy, and understanding. Vulnerability connects us on a deeper level, creating a shared experience of humanity. It breaks down societal stigmas and allows for the creation of a more compassionate and inclusive society. In reading Dan's story, you may have felt how this beautiful community provided just this experience for one another.

Vulnerability connects us on a deeper level.

MOVING INTO THE BODY

Our deeper work together is about to begin. We will be touching on what is happening inside our bodies as we enter part 2, and we may begin to sense that we are filled with many attachment memories. It is important as we do this inner work that we learn how to create some space in our lives to be with ourselves and our bodies in new ways. The more we slow down and begin listening to our inner world, the more we create inner space. I started doing this work by taking on less in my career and slowing down enough to really pay attention to what was going on inside me.

We refer to this process as coming into contact with our inborn capacity for *interoception* (how we sense the internal state of our body) and building *inner attunement* (welcoming whatever we discover). For many of us, our parents weren't in touch with these capacities and therefore couldn't share them with us. This kind of inner sensitivity is the missing developmental link we will begin to foster now. As we tune into what we are sensing in our bodies, we start to welcome and be with our *whole selves*.

We'll also be learning the science behind how we store our memories inside our hearts, bellies, and muscles, and together we will carefully tend to these memories in new ways. This can bring up things we might not be prepared for. Those of us who have more avoidant protectors might have had to detach from challenging feelings, while those who are more anxious might have explosive sensations emerge. As we've just learned, the *supportive presence* of others can be incredibly helpful in anchoring us and holding our experiences. As you familiarize yourself with the practices in part 2, you may first find yourself reading to learn about the process as you deepen your understanding. Then rereading to begin practicing this new way of being present with your deeper self. Then rereading again and again to deepen the work. First, a toe in the water, and then gradually immersing yourself in the whole healing pool. At the same time, I imagine you will be drawn to find companions on the journey. I trust I will have the privilege of being one of them along the way. What was wounded in relationship can now start to heal in relationship.

2

COMING HOME
TO OUR BODIES

CHAPTER 4

THE ETERNALLY PRESENT PAST

I n the previous chapter, we spent time with Dan and our therapy group. Without much feeling, he told us about how lonely he had felt as a kid, and we listened and held space for him just as he was. When we are received this way, we begin to feel safe. And safety makes room for vulnerability. For Dan, this meant that he gradually began to feel his body's sensations. At one point, as he was speaking to us, he paused for a quick moment and put his hand on his belly, although I wasn't sure he was even aware of this gesture. Then he continued sharing about the loneliness, and I asked gently, "What are you feeling in your body as you share these memories?" He was quiet for a moment and then said tentatively, "Maybe a tightness in my chest. And a gnawing pain in my gut. I feel like I'm breathing a little faster." He seemed reluctant to go on, but eventually said softly, "I've also got kind of a spiky pain in my eyes. It feels like I could cry."

"I wonder when your body may have felt just like this before?" I asked.

He looked into my eyes tentatively and then said, "I see myself at maybe four. And I look really, really sad."

Dan may or may not have been conscious of the sensations in his body or what they were communicating before I asked him the question, but it was clear that something was drawing his body's attention to how disconnected he had felt as a child and perhaps now as well. In the weeks that followed, supported by me and his fellow group mates, Dan became more adept at tracking the sensations in his body.

Dan was developing the ability to attend to the signals his body was offering him. He was literally building new neural pathways—actual connections in his brain—that make what we call *interoception* (listening to our bodies) possible. And this ability was quickly becoming a vital gateway to healing the pain and fear he had carried since childhood. As Dan felt the embodied presence of the neglected child inside of him, we could be with him and provide the comfort and attention he had needed when he was little but had simply not been available to him, given how overtaxed his family had been.

In this chapter, we will explore how you can develop and deepen your capacity for bodily awareness, a crucial first step toward healing the attachment wounds so many of us carry. First, it will help to understand something about the connection between our bodily sensations and our earlier experiences and how this shapes the way we think, feel, behave, and relate in the present.

Our memories are held in multiple systems in our bodies. With each new experience in our lives, we sometimes encode the narrative memory of "what happened," but we always encode the sensations we felt in our bellies, hearts, muscles, skin, autonomic nervous systems, and more when we first had the experience. When we recall these past experiences, these sensations return whether we are conscious of them or not. These felt sense experiences are a powerful form of "remembering." Whenever I am on my way to meet a certain close and dear friend, the memories of all our good times together converge in my body, often before I have even registered how excited I am to see her. I feel a warmth in my chest, my muscles feel relaxed, and my digestion is easy as I anticipate how good it will feel to hug her. These embodied recollections are called *implicit memories*. We are making these kinds of memories all the time, throughout our lives, without conscious awareness. When these past experiences reawaken in us, they feel as though they are happening right now. Even as I am writing about lunch with my friend, I feel all the pleasant sensations in my body. Bonnie Badenoch calls these implicit memories, which have no time stamp, "the eternally present past."

Most of us think of memory as the stories we tell about certain events in our lives. "I remember when we went to Disneyland for the first time." "I remember how sad I was when Grandpa died." These stories usually have a beginning, a middle, and an end, and we are certain that they happened in the past. We call these stories *explicit memories*, and we begin forming them around age two or three. Only if they are connected to the implicit part of the memory do they have any feeling to them. That disconnection between implicit and explicit is why Dan could initially share his childhood story in such a flat, unemotional way.

When we are born, the parts of our brain required to make explicit memories aren't yet connected with each other, so all of our earliest attachment experiences are held implicitly, in the body, as sensations. Throughout our lives, we will continue to make implicit memories of all our emotionally meaningful experiences and all the cultural and familial patterns that we swim in every day. In fact, because we don't have to be paying conscious attention to encode an implicit memory, we will make exponentially more implicit memories than explicit ones, which do require conscious attention. Researcher Andreas Riener estimates that we are taking in about eleven million bits of implicit information each second while processing only about forty to fifty bits of information explicitly. That's really astonishing. It means the way we feel, think, behave, and relate is far more influenced by what we are carrying implicitly than what we consciously remember.

Most important, these implicit memories continuously shape the way we perceive everything around us. With each implicit memory that emerges, it is as if we put on a pair of colored glasses that tint our view of the present with the feelings and perceptions that took root in us from past experience. If we were often afraid as children, when these memories are awake now, all the physical sensations of fear in our bodies can make the world of relationships feel like a very scary place.

If I had parents who were highly anxious when they held me, my body will still have responses to their inability to be truly present to me. Lots of things began to happen in my body then and continue to happen now when those memories are reawakened. My belly, which is a second brain, is very sensitive to experiences that are safe or not safe and may tighten or get queasy. My heart (literally, a third brain which senses the quality of connection) may beat more rapidly or my chest may clench. My system feels it has to be on guard because there is no one to receive me with calm and loving attention, so my muscles will tense and my autonomic nervous system will go on high alert. Even my skin will have a response to contact that doesn't feel soothing, maybe shrinking away or burning or craving more contact.

All of these sensations were poured into my infant body as a single implicit memory that begins to generate a perception that this world isn't a safe place, people won't take care of me, and possibly, there is something wrong with me because the people I depend on can't offer me a feeling of loving connection. None of this will be conveyed in words or concepts. The memory is made up entirely of sensations that result in a compelling felt sense in the body that begins to build an implicit knowing about the true nature of how things will be for me. The more often this experience is repeated, the more convinced my system becomes that *This is the way it is*. Eventually, as my brain matures to the point that it can make up stories, I will create narratives that match these feelings. The sad result is that when we are grown, these memories of the past are so deeply ingrained in our being that we can't experience ourselves, the world, and other people through any other lens. Yet, as I have said, history isn't destiny. When we are in the company of someone who can offer nonjudgmental holding and warm attentive care, these implicit perceptions can change. But for this to happen, we need to be able to reenter the felt sense of the memory. This is where *interoception* (sensing what is happening in our bodies) and *inner attunement* (extending welcome to what is awakening in our bodies) become the all-important foundation for healing. This is what we are going to practice in the next part of this chapter.

ACCESSING YOUR RICH STOREHOUSE OF EMBODIED MEMORIES

Our families aren't the only place we develop profound attachment patterns. In elementary school, we spend nine months a year, five days a week, in relationship with mostly one person. In school, the teacher is in charge of us and we are at their mercy, which gives these relationships a lot of emotional power. Our sensitive little selves become inwardly aware of every nuance of that connection. No matter how many or how few explicit memories I have, my body holds a whole galaxy of implicit memories from each of those formative years.

I started thinking about the power of school relationships because Laurene, one of my clients, took me back into her experience of elementary school where she had felt deeply uncared for by her third-grade teacher, Mrs. Heard.

Laurene is now forty-five, but as I listened to her words, I felt like I was with her all those many years ago in her grade school classroom. She described how every day Mrs. Heard greeted her students with the same disapproving, unsmiling face. All of her students believed she simply didn't like kids. I asked Laurene how the memories of her teacher were showing up in her body. She told me her upper thighs were getting tense because she wanted to run away. She also told me she felt a little queasiness in her belly, with her breath starting to come a little more quickly and her chest feeling achy. As we sat together listening to Laurene's eight-year-old self, she began to sob. It seemed that a misery she had never been able to express for decades was now pouring out. As I spoke gently and extended my hand to her, together we embraced her "Little Me." As we felt her with us more and more, Laurene's story rushed forward, and her body gradually began to calm.

The next time Laurene came in, she told me that being with that school experience had somehow also brought her into her fifth-grade classroom and it felt important to be with that experience as well. I didn't know what to expect, but as her face relaxed into a quiet smile, I could already see that fifth grade had been very different from third grade. She began by telling me, "I wholeheartedly wish that every child had at least one teacher like Miss Forest! She was tough because she really wanted us to learn, but she also saw each one of us as an individual. She clearly loved us and went out of her way to let us know we were valuable to her. For me, this was magic because none of it was happening at home." Her body was clearly and easily remembering the visceral joy of that year. It was sweet to feel how much Miss Forest was now one of Laurene's inner anchors.

One of the things our elementary school experience does is set in place, in our bodies, anticipations about how things will be for us in groups where someone is in charge. Implicit memory is like water. It spreads out and finds all the places that are roughly similar to the original event. This includes school at any age, of course, but also many work settings, experiences volunteering, and often even social groups where there is a predetermined hierarchy. As we sat with these two experiences, it became clear to Laurene that because of her early experience, when she is new to a group, her body prepares her for Mrs. Heard while hoping she will encounter Miss Forest. She is wisely tense, watchful, and slightly short of breath until she gets the lay of the land. Once there is enough safety, the whole Miss Forest experience starts to surface in her body, and she is free to enjoy the presence of all the new people. This is the power of the implicit world that is always with us.

NURTURING INTEROCEPTION

It is worth saying again that what was wounded in relationship can heal in relationship. This is true at all levels, both in terms of the healing that can take place in our relationships with others and the healing that comes from our relationship with ourselves, specifically with our bodies. With this in mind, one of the first connections we want to nurture is our capacity for *interoception*, which is our ability to be present with our bodies—to listen to what they are telling us without seeking to change anything.

> What was wounded in relationship can heal in relationship.

As we begin to practice interoception together, it is so important for us to be gentle with ourselves. Many of us didn't have what we needed in our early years to develop this capacity, so we may feel quite estranged from our body's immediate sensations. If our parents didn't have the opportunity to develop this ability when they were young, they were likely not able to pass it on to us.

The other hindrance to awareness of physical sensations is cultural. When our left hemispheres are dominant, as they are for so many of us now living in our increasingly fast-paced, "you've got to stay on your toes" culture, the neural pathways that connect us with moment-to-moment sensitivity to our bodies' current state are out of reach. My constant push toward busyness and achievement was my system's attempt to protect me by keeping me unaware of my body's signals of pain and fear. But when the inner distress became too great, the sensations broke through in dramatic ways that sent me to the ER. We might also recall from the last chapter that as Dan slowed down and was embraced by the group, his hand automatically moved to his belly, the sign that he was becoming more and more connected to his bodily sensations. There is so much wisdom in our bodies. They hold so much experience.

Practice: The Brain in Our Heart

With this practice, we will begin to visit some of the central systems in our bodies that store implicit memory, just being present for and listening to what they have to share with us when we recall key people from our past. In this practice we will focus on nonfamily members as a way to ease into the often tender or vulnerable memories of relationship that may dwell within us. You can do this practice with your listening partner, a friend, or your therapist. There is also a recorded version of all the meditations in this book at jessicabaumlmhc.com/safe-meditations. Or you may simply read the instructions and respond in your journal.

Let's begin by slowly and gently placing a hand on our heart/chest area. The sensations we experience in our hearts are spread out across our chest because there are rosette-like neural centers in our thoracic cavity that are intertwined with the forty thousand or so neurons that make up our heart brain. We might call them *roses of attachment,* since our heart brains are dedicated to remembering experiences of connection. If we have had many warm, safe relationships in our lives, when we recall them, sensations of openness and fullness may arise here. If we have had a few or many relationships that scared us or in which we felt abandoned or ignored, sensations of clenching, emptiness, or pain may come when we remember these encounters. For either type of memory, the felt sense that happened in our hearts with the original experience will wake up in our bodies when we return to the memory. We will come back to this practice as we move through this chapter to visit other central parts of our body that also store implicit memory, namely our muscles and our bellies, but for now we begin with our heart.

1. Bringing our warm, receptive attention to the contact between our hand and our heart, let us just wait and listen, not trying to pull anything up. Now we can begin to recall our relationship with a teacher or a coach, a friend's mother or a neighbor that felt particularly nourishing. We might see this person's face in our mind's eye or hear their voice—or we might simply feel their presence.

2. As we spend some time with this person, we might begin to notice sensations arising in our heart and chest. We can pause to enjoy this felt sense. We might also hear some single words emerging as if they are coming directly from this place of contact. Just listen and receive. It is possible that the sensations will be very mild or even nonexistent at first. If our systems are not used to being conscious of our bodily sensations, perhaps nothing much will happen. If so, see if it is possible to receive this without judgment. We are not responsible for how our neural circuits were supported or neglected during our development. Beginning together right here and now with where we are, slowly we will find

that these neural pathways are receiving the attention they need, so they can gradually bring our bodily sensations into awareness.

3. When we have spent some time here, we can take a little deeper breath and thank the person who arrived whether they brought sensations of warm connection or not. Now we can slowly release the contact between our heart and hand and just pause for a bit.

4. When we feel ready, we can bring our hand back into contact with our chest and now call to mind someone with whom we had a difficult, painful, or frightening connection. We can do this slowly and stay with this memory only for as long as it feels okay to continue. The presence of a listening partner or friend can help us expand our depth of receptivity as they lend us their nervous system to help us hold whatever arises.

5. As we spend some time with this person, we can again notice what sensations arise in our heart and chest, along with some words that come spontaneously to describe the physical feelings—be it words such as "tight," "empty," "aching," "cold,"

"collapsed," or something entirely different. It may be tempting to feel a strong preference for the pleasant feelings you have just experienced recalling someone whom you felt safe with and to want to turn away from these more painful sensations. If this is true for you, try to focus on the beauty of the fact that your heart finally feels safe to share the truth of its remembered experience. This felt sense may come and go or not come at all. Just being with whatever unfolds, with as little judgment as possible, is right where we need to be.

6. After being with this person and these sensations (or not) for a little while, taking a little deeper breath and thanking them for their presence, gently bring your hand away from your chest as you release this memory.

7. As a way to honor the experiences you have been recalling with the two individuals in this practice, it can be very helpful to spend some time sharing with your listening partner or friend, or writing in your journal about the experience, paying special attention to exploring how it was to focus on physical sensations rather than the mental stories we've made up about them.

If we return to this practice daily for a while, our connection to the deep experience and wisdom in our hearts will emerge more and more. Even if we have been strangers to our bodies for a long time, our offer of contact will awaken a response, bit by bit. We began with the heart because many people seem to feel sensations there more easily than in their bellies or muscles. Now we will continue by focusing on another area of our body that holds many implicit memories. When you feel you want to end the practice, gently bring yourself back into the room. Slowly open your eyes and notice a few things in the room to help ground you back into your day.

WHAT OUR MUSCLES REMEMBER

Another bodily sensation that may become accessible to awareness can originate in our muscles, so let's go there next. The state of our muscles is powerfully connected to whether we are having a neuroception of safety or not. As our bodies prepare to respond to a threat, various groups of muscles tighten to prepare us to fight or flee. Or if we become so frightened that we feel helpless, our muscles may shut down as we begin to collapse. On the other hand, when we feel safe, our muscles soften and relax. We may reserve a small amount of tension in our muscles for playful exchanges with someone we enjoy being with, or experience a more complete relaxation of all of our muscles for quiet meditation or talk with a loved person. Feeling no need to defend ourselves with people we hold near and dear, we relax.

Every implicit memory we make encodes the presence or absence of tension in our muscles similar to the way we experienced sensations in our heart. So now we can return to the above practice and once again think of the two people we invited when we explored sensations in our heart. As you do the exercise, this time see how your muscles respond to the presence of these two people. Rather than placing your hand on any particular muscle, you can simply sit with your whole body and see what you notice. As I remember my relationship with a co-worker who was unpredictably unpleasant, I begin to feel tension in my neck, as though my muscles want to suck my head down into my shoulders. Or I notice that my thighs become tight as though they are preparing to run. If I shift my attention to my good friend down the street, my upper legs let go immediately and my shoulder and neck muscles slowly relax, allowing my neck to lengthen and my head to emerge. It is not a metaphor to say that our muscles remember. Exploring our physiological condition as we recall different people or experiences in our lives is how we make contact with the felt sense of what happened to us in the past.

Let's go step-by-step through the practice we did with the heart, only this time listen to our muscles. As we finish, taking time to write about it or talk with an anchor will help us deepen

> It is not a metaphor to say that our muscles remember.

into our understanding of this kind of remembering. With every practice, we are nurturing our capacity for *interoception*, and with every offer of welcoming sensation, we are fostering *inner attunement*.

Each of us will have certain kinds of embodied memories that are easier to access than others. I seem to be very sensitive to what happens in my heart and my autonomic nervous system, while others tell me that their muscles or bellies have the loudest voices. One isn't better than the other. It's just such a rich exploration to find out how our systems speak to us most clearly and easily. Here, we're just experimenting with some of the main systems to get better acquainted with the voices of sensation in our unique bodies.

OUR BELLY'S WISE VOICE

Now let's spend some time with our belly. This truly is our second brain, as it is often called. With somewhere between one hundred and five hundred million neurons and using the same neurotransmitters as the brain in our skull for communication, it is a sophisticated system for responding to danger and for remembering the sensations that belong to every implicit memory. These neural pathways extend from the notch at the bottom of our throat to our anus, twenty-six feet of responsive wisdom and memory. If my belly knots up or there's constriction above my belly button or some butterflies when my hypercritical aunt arrives, those same sensations can come when I remember her. They are a living connection to my experience of her.

Our bellies are just as intimately connected with digesting relationships as they are with digesting food. Consequently, our stomachs are as apt to become upset in some way if we encounter someone who hurts or scares us as if we eat food that makes us sick. It is no wonder that digestive issues are extremely common if we have experienced attachment wounds.

When I met Jeremy, one of the first things he told me was that he had a swarm of butterflies in his stomach coming into my office for the first time, and wasn't sure he could stay. His honesty warmed me, and I assured him I understood. I said softly, "You will always be free to leave at any moment if you need to, no questions asked. And you'll always be free to return." I believe he stopped breathing for a moment, then let out an enormous sigh as he placed his hand on his belly. We were quiet for a moment before he said, "I believe a few of them have landed." We both smiled broadly and began.

He told me he couldn't remember the last time his stomach felt settled for a whole day. "Even in childhood?" I asked.

"Especially then. I never ate breakfast before going to school because I always felt like I would throw up," he said, continuing with "Is that normal?"

"Well, it certainly means something," I replied.

Jeremy went on to describe how his parents got into yelling fights every day. "I thought they hated each other, but they also hugged and kissed in front of me. I was terribly confused." As he said that, he bent over a little, his hand on his belly. We paused there to notice the rising tension in his stomach, and he said, "That was the worst, never knowing what to expect."

As we continued, it was clear that his belly had been responding to the perpetual but unpredictable lack of safety in his home since he was small. His belly's voice was so loud and consistent that it was as though he was living back in his family home most days. Any hint of uncertainty awakened the memories that agitated his belly. Now its waves of sensation were becoming our guide as we moved toward healing the traumatic implicit memories that continued to torment his life.

The sensations in your belly may not be as dramatic as Jeremy's, but doing the practice we did with our hearts and substituting a gentle hand on our bellies can help us begin to listen to what this wise brain is whispering when we revisit the two people we have been following. As we call the first person, the nourishing one, to mind and heart, we can begin by asking our bellies where on its long path it would like our hand to rest, anywhere between the notch at the bottom of our neck to our lower abdomen. Then we can just arrive and listen to whatever sensations may come. When we call on the second person, the one who hurt or scared us, we can ask again where our hand might be most supportive and then wait to see what arises. Following the practice step-by-step and then sharing with our listening person or journal can be an important movement toward developing a living relationship with this ongoing source of wisdom.

I chose these three streams of sensation—heart, muscles, and belly—for our practice of interoception because they carry such a wealth of information and provide such reliable roads back to the implicit memories that are asking for healing. Doing these daily for a while will help strengthen your capacity for interoception from a whisper to a reliable voice. As that happens, you will likely also begin to notice the response of other streams of information—your breathing patterns, your heart rate, tension in places like your jaws and around your eyes, and so much more. This increasing sensitivity is in preparation for what we will do in chapter 5—get in touch with our early attachment experiences, which live only in the sensations in our bodies.

TOUCHED AND AWAKENED

As we go on through our days, a current experience will sometimes activate older implicit memories from earlier times in our lives. When our implicit memories are touched, they reawaken the sensations we felt in our bodies long ago and change our perception of the present moment. Because my father ignored me, sometimes when someone turns their back on me now, my stomach tightens and my heart beats fast as my whole body relives the panic I felt as a child when I was ignored.

Because awakened implicit memories always feel like they're happening right now, I used to believe that these intense feelings were entirely because of the person who had just turned away. Many of us, myself included, have pointed a finger at a loved one and said, "You're triggering me!"—placing all the blame on some behavior that they are doing that is causing us to feel a particular way. As I was working with Jo, I learned that what was going on inside me was actually partly old memories coming to the surface. As I really understood this concept, it made it possible for me to embrace, hold, and tend to my inner experience in a new way. I have learned to slow down, invite Jo to be with the Little Me who endured so much abandonment, and help this young one feel our loving presence with her now.

I also have less of a need to blame my partner or others if I feel pain because I can now see more clearly when the pain is something that already lived inside of me, long before they said something or made a gesture that caused me to remember it. Instead of the anger or panic or collapse that I used to feel, I am finding I can be curious about what is happening with the person who just turned away from me. This makes room for us to possibly repair what just happened rather than escalate into an even more painful disruption. I can't always do all of this, but at the very least, I am aware that these waves of big feelings most often have roots in the past and are not based only on what is happening in the present. That alone lets my system take a pause before responding. This is truly life-changing.

Waves of big feelings most often have roots in the past.

Often when something happens in the present moment that awakens our bodies' memory of a past event, we say we have been "triggered." For me there is something violent about this word—indeed the awakening of painful old feelings can have a distinctly aggressive flavor. At the same time, it seems to me that there can be a feeling of shame attached to this word, as though there is something wrong with emotions being activated in a given moment—as if we should, in fact, fear our emotions rather than try to be with them. This word—and the intonation we use with it—can also become a weapon of blame we aim toward a person we see as the cause for our upset. But here's the thing. When these old traumatic memories wake up, they do not come alive in order to injure us. They arise so that we may seek healing. Whenever they come alive in our bodies, they make us available to receive what psychotherapist Bruce Ecker calls a "disconfirming experience." As he would say, these awakening implicit memories in our bodies provide the opportunity for us to receive what we needed at the time of the original injury but simply wasn't available to us. If we were frightened, we needed safety. If we were sad, we needed comfort. If we felt ashamed, we needed complete acceptance. You can learn more about Ecker's work in the Wisdom Notes section at the end of this book.

When my father's pain led him to turn away from me, what I needed was someone to be with me, to acknowledge my pain, and to fill up the hole left by my father's absence. Someone to disconfirm the message that I wasn't worth his attention. For this old wound to heal now, I need to be in contact with the embodied pain of my father's abandonment while in the company of someone whose heart hears my pain and who wants me to know that they are with me now. That I am safe. For me, this has been Jo, Alan, a couple of other anchors, and sometimes even just the memory of my grandmother. Over time, it has become less painful for me to think of my father's absence because the neural nets holding that experience are now bathed in the presence of these loving hearts.

The awakening of implicit memory is an opportunity for healing, and as such, perhaps we can use some word other than *triggered* to describe the arrival of these sensations. Bonnie Badenoch has suggested words like *touched and awakened* or *activated* as ways of more gently, yet proactively, receiving the arrival of embodied implicit memories. Let's see what happens in our bodies when we play around with these words.

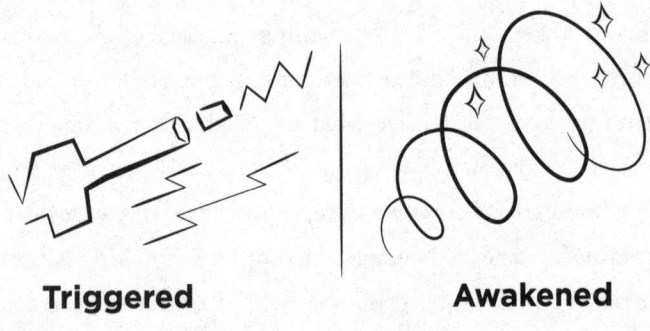

Triggered   **Awakened**

When I was learning about awakened states, someone suggested I draw a picture of what comes to mind when I hear the word *triggered* and the word *awakened*. This is what came up for me. The word *triggered* felt like a gun with rough edges to it. It even had a feeling of violence, reactivity, and blame attached to it. The word *awakened* had a feeling of growth, evolving, and progressing in a process. Over time, I also noticed that when I approached my body's implicit memories with the understanding that they were an opportunity for healing, it felt as though they arrived a little bit more gently. It may sound strange to imagine that a different word could do this, but it was more than that. I was actually getting into a different relationship with my body's memories. I started seeing implicit memories as helpers rather than as enemies.

With that, we're ready to move together into our next exploration, our attachment experiences as young ones. It will be helpful to continue doing the exercises we did in this chapter to further strengthen your capacity for interoception as well as develop a deeper relationship

> I started seeing implicit memories as helpers rather than as enemies.

with your precious body, guided by growing inner attunement. Everything we are sharing here is meant to become a lifelong practice of intimacy with your inner world made possible by a growing community of trusted people with whom you do this work.

CHAPTER 5

HEALING OUR YOUNGER SELVES

The more I learned from relational neuroscience about how memories are held in our bodies, the more I started to incorporate interoception into my practice, supporting my clients in strengthening their connection with the neural circuits that could help them become more aware of sensations. Often, during our sessions, as they talked with me about whatever struggles they were having, I would ask what they were experiencing in their bodies. Their responses taught me so much about the intricate connection between the mind and the body when it comes to memory. We would pause and wait for their muscles, hearts, bellies, or autonomic nervous systems to speak. As they became aware of persistent tension in a particular muscle group or the felt sense of needing to pull away or an ache deep in their bellies or hearts, I would ask, "I wonder when your body might have felt just like this before?" My role in this experience was to have no preconceived idea about what would happen next, just holding an open space for us to discover where their body's wisdom might carry us. It is true that sometimes we also discovered that these sensations were about a stressful moment at work or muscle pain from a particularly strenuous trip to the gym. But as long as we held a receptive space for whatever wanted to emerge, we would often arrive at the memory of an experience from much earlier in their lives. These embodied feelings became our guides, helping us get in touch with memories that needed healing.

RELATIONSHIPS ON AUTOPILOT

As I'm writing about this, Corrie and James come to mind. They came into therapy because they found themselves having the same miserable argument just about every day. The subject of their conflict might vary and also which of the two was the one to initiate the touchy topic, but the pattern was always the same. For example, one or the other would make some sort of definite statement—"It's going to be too hot for the camellias tomorrow" or "Chrissie [their daughter] doesn't want to go on the field trip tomorrow." The other's brow would raise. A silence would hang in the air. And then: "I think the camellias are pretty hardy" or "Well, she has to go." The originator of the statement would then counter with more evidence. "I looked it up online and when it gets to ninety degrees, that's too much for them" or "She says she's been having a fight with her friend Betsy and doesn't want to be on the bus with her." At that point, often one of them would simply change the subject. But many times, it would go on: "You always disagree with me" or "You are the most stubborn human!" Defensiveness and yelling would then ensue until they had exhausted themselves and someone wound up leaving the room.

They both thought these arguments were silly, petty, and generally a waste of time because, ultimately, they usually came to a good solution together. One of the most touching things they told me was that, even though these disagreements seemed minor, they were ruining the quality of their relationship and hurting their kids. They had read a bunch of books, done some therapy, and tried every technique to stop the cycle, but it felt to both of them as if they just went on automatic pilot with each other sometimes.

It was clear to me that Corrie and James really loved each other, but it was also clear that they felt helpless about changing this pattern. Sitting with couples for years has taught me that this usually means an old implicit pattern is being evoked by certain circumstances. What I have learned is that techniques don't work, so in order to alter the underlying pattern, we need to go deeper. I asked if any of this felt familiar from the past.

James flinched immediately in response to my question. He said that he and his brothers often fled the house because of their parents' constant fighting. Corrie nodded her head and shared that my question immediately summoned in her the pain of watching her parents get into long, intense arguments about nothing. She said, "When James and I got together, we vowed we would never ever do that to our kids." Their bowed heads and drooping shoulders spoke of the deep shame they both felt about repeating a pattern they knew all too well from their childhoods.

Then James asked the crucial question: "We know what we don't want to do. We're reasonably intelligent people. Other therapists have given us techniques to stop this stupid bickering and fighting, and yet we can't do it for even a day. Once we start these conflicts, it's like getting on a train that only goes one way and there's no getting off. What's wrong with us?"

My honest answer was "Nothing is wrong with you."

The truth is that the relationships that surround us in our earliest days can instill *core patterns of connecting* in us that we will act out for the rest of our lives (until we do the work to heal and change them). Because we don't remember those early days explicitly, it can be hard to believe this is true, but yes, our initial attachments really are that impactful, and as we move through life, the patterns are continually reaffirmed and strengthened.

What we carry is complex. We have some patterns created by our embodied response to how others in our family were relating to us and each other. (Did we feel safe, scared, endangered?) We have internalized the actual patterns of their relationships with us. (Were we ignored, hovered over, listened to?) And we also have the ways in which our family members related to each other. (Was it with respect, with criticism, with domination?)

Pause for Reflection

With your journal or possibly a listening partner, ask yourself a couple of questions. *How did my body respond to the way people in my family related to me?* Multiple scenarios are likely to arise if you sit with this for a while. In most families, there are several common patterns of relating. Make note of each one and how your body responded. We can be with this question slowly and return to it often. When you feel ready, we can also ask, *What happened in my body when I watched family members relate to each other?* Remember as well that we are just as affected by what we witness as by what happens to us directly. As you ask this question, notice which groups come to mind—parents with each other, parents with each sibling, interactions between siblings, and more. These questions are just beginning to reveal the ocean of attachment in which you swam every day as a child.

There are two vitally important things to understand about what we carry implicitly from our early years. These deeply ingrained implicit patterns create embodied expectations in us about how all relationships will be for us. These are deeply rooted in our unconscious. We come into every new encounter preloaded with anticipations that match whatever terms of engagement we learned in our families. Does attaching to someone mean becoming subservient to them? Does closeness come with a willingness to be ignored? Does becoming connected mean that the other person is unpredictable, sometimes attentive and sometimes lost in their own world? Does it include misunderstandings that are quickly repaired? We each have our own expectations. It is likely that some of them will be nourishing, and some will carry a warning label. Corrie and James both told me that they absolutely knew their parents loved each other, no matter how angry and mean they were. They had also seen these parents be able to repair the miserable rifts, and reported they were, in fact, still arguing and still married. In the midst of misery, there are also sometimes powerful messages that give us the hope to seek closeness with others. At the same time, Corrie and James had lived in environments that frightened them and led their inner worlds to expect that all closeness would include ongoing altercations.

The second thing that is so important to understand is that when these old implicit memories are awakened, they generate automatic behaviors about one hundred times faster than we can think what to do next and possibly change our response. Our implicit pathways are one hundred times faster than our thinking, deciding circuits. This is why just knowledge of the issue or relational techniques couldn't help Corrie and James stop their arguing. This is why all of us can point to times when we are bewildered by having said or done something we swore we would never do or say. What James said about getting on a speeding train is the perfect metaphor for how our activated implicit memories keep generating the relational nightmares we most want to avoid.

As I explained all of this to Corrie and James, their shoulders relaxed some and they were able to make eye contact with each other again. "There isn't anything wrong with you," I said once more. "It's just the way our human brains work. The best news is that your bodies hold everything we need to touch into these old patterns and heal them."

As we move into this chapter together, this is our pathway, too. Our Little Me and the relationships they have experienced live inside our bodies, holding both painful and joyful memories of attachment. Together, we will begin attuning to the stories they're trying to share with us. Touching the nourishing experiences strengthens them, and they become more powerful inner anchors for us. Spending time with the painful and frightening relationships can infuse these memories with presence and care, transforming them from developmental traumas into healed oases of security and safety.

I want to be one of the anchors for you through these unfolding experiences, and I also hope you find a way to begin to invite more and more safe people in to hold your attachment wounds with you. It is especially sweet when two people can do this for each other. The reason another person—a trusted anchor—is so helpful in healing these earlier wounds is because, when we were little, we needed our primary caregiver to be truly present with us, and when they were not, we had no choice but to store the pain and fear in our bodies until we could find someone who could hold our pains and our joys, someone who could fully witness us. If we didn't have this when we were young, when we finally find it in our here and now, what was once "no one is there for me" becomes "when I reach out to my anchors, people do show up." We are able to fully integrate our internal experiences and build and strengthen our neural systems so that we may move forward more securely. This internal shift changes everything, as we will see.

Other kinds of anchors may also become important for us, too. Sometimes we know our early traumas were agonizing, and sometimes, as we approach them, they turn out to be much more painful than we imagined. These are the times to seek a therapist as a companion, one who can deeply hold the sacred territory of early attachment.

When our Little Me received an early attachment wound, all of the pain and fear were tucked away deep inside us with the hopes that we might never experience that original wound again. Keeping our awareness away from the wound is a form of self-protection. The sadly ironic thing is that even when we go to great lengths to not feel our wounds, they continue speaking to us in many subtle ways. They often draw us to partners who feel familiar to us subconsciously, or when we're in a relationship, we experience conflict that awakens memories that have being lying dormant for a long time.

Corrie and James had developed a good deal of clarity about why just understanding the reasons for their arguing wasn't going to stop them from repeating painful patterns from their childhoods. As they discovered, often the first step to healing our early wounds is to become aware of the ways that our Little Me may have embedded painful memories in our bodies. The next time they came to see me, they were ready to begin this deeper work. I asked them if they would be willing to return to their most recent argument to see what we could discover. James volunteered to begin, since he felt he'd started the whole thing, and it had been a particularly juvenile and stupid fight. "I had been doing some gardening work in the backyard, and when I stepped into the kitchen to get a glass of water, Corrie said, 'Please wipe your feet.' Without so much as a thought, I barked at her. 'They're not dirty.'"

I asked if we could pause right there. We took a breath and I asked James about the feeling in his body when he heard Corrie say, "Please wipe your feet."

His face flushed as I said the words. "My belly gets into a knot immediately when you say that. And my biceps and thighs tighten."

I quietly asked, "I wonder if there is a time earlier in life when your body felt just like this?"

He closed his eyes and then he said, "I'm seeing the thousands of times my mother got furious when we dragged mud in the house. She chased us with a big metal spoon and really hurt us sometimes when she caught us."

Corrie's face softened almost to tears. I said gently, "I am so sorry. Can we be with that little boy who was so scared and so hurt?"

"He just wants to run."

"Can we run with him?"

He opened his eyes and said, "You're persistent, aren't you."

"No child should be alone with that kind of fear and pain."

Everything got very quiet, and I knew the young one inside James had heard and felt us wanting to bring him to safety and comfort. James shared some more about his mother's unpredictability and violence, and we paused frequently to be with the feelings in his body that belonged to the child who had endured this regular abuse. Gradually, he felt his muscles letting go, his breath slowing, and his belly growing more relaxed, all signs that this child was taking us in. He was accompanied now by three adults—Corrie, the adult James, and me—who had experienced the embodied truth of his story and were dedicated to keeping him safe in this present moment.

Corrie told her husband how touched she was by what had happened. "You've never let me know how bad it was, sweetheart. You always made it sound like a bit of a joke, a little bit of slapstick comedy where your mother was just a little rough with you all sometimes to keep you in line. I had no idea you were so scared and so hurt by your mother when you were a kid. No wonder you jumped down my throat when I said those words. I'm sure I sounded impatient with you because I was fatigued by all the cleaning and tidying up we have to do here, but I didn't mean to sound angry. I wasn't angry with you."

"I don't think I realized how bad it was either until just now. I actually felt what it used to feel like," he said. We talked about how James's joking ways and defensive responses were his protectors, keeping the fear and pain as far away as possible, while they were also unintentionally repeating the very patterns he had seen with his parents. And that is where we ended our time together that day.

The next time they came in, Corrie was ready to go deeper into her experience of wanting to shove James away when he snapped at her. And so it went. And yet their deep love for each other coupled with their desire to be the best possible parents carried them, week after week, through this difficult yet rewarding work. Their compassion for each other grew and they began to feel safer together. The inevitable arguments became fewer and further between—and they were no longer automatic. Just as a quarrel was about to start, one of them would sometimes be able to ask for a pause to be with the Little Me they were getting to know. While it would be many months of ongoing work with their little ones before this new pattern of being safer together settled in, their kids were already beginning to notice a change.

REBECCA'S AWAKENING

Not every passage through healing goes as easily as it did with Corrie and James. Rebecca was in her mid-fifties when she came to see me because she felt like she was falling apart. At work, it seemed her boss had developed a habit of ignoring her, almost like she wasn't there. If he did pay attention, it was to criticize her. She'd heard that his daughter was ill, and she thought perhaps that was why he seemed so different, but that didn't seem to calm her panicky feelings. Even though work was hard, she had at least found a safe haven at home with her longtime boyfriend. But now, for reasons she couldn't understand, and he couldn't talk about, he seemed to be losing interest in her. When she asked him what was wrong, he just said, "Nothing." All of this was so upsetting that it was leading to some serious digestive issues. Some days, her appetite was just gone, and she was having trouble sleeping.

That first day, she said to me, "I feel like I'm losing my mind. I shouldn't be this upset. I'm not like this every day, but it's often enough that I'm scared."

I listened and said, "I believe you're exactly as upset as you need to be, but it may not all be about now, although the changes in these two important men in your life would of course be upsetting. Sometimes difficult situations in our present life wake up old memories and bring on incredibly intense emotions and feelings in our bodies. Sometimes especially in our bellies."

She said, "I don't know what that could be. I come from a normal family where nobody ever hit me or hurt me." I listened as she told me about her early life. There were many sweet memories from elementary school days, but she also had an older sister who'd gotten cancer when Rebecca was an infant and passed away by the time Rebecca was a toddler. She had no explicit memories from the time, but said she felt a tightness in her throat and belly telling me about it.

Over the next few weeks, we got to know each other, developing trust and closeness. We talked about how implicit memories show up in the body, about the Little Me that we all have, and how painful experiences in our childhood can fundamentally change our felt sense of the world. The growing safety between us began to make way for the big feelings that had brought Rebecca to see me. The next time she came in, she was in a great deal of pain because of her boss and her boyfriend. And, once again, mad at herself for having such big feelings.

While the growing upset in her home and work lives was making her body feel tight all over, these sensations were soon overwhelmed by a pain in her belly. I asked if she could put her hand on the spot where it hurt the most. She put her hand right over her belly button and the sensations immediately escalated, first to nausea and then to a feeling of terrifying emptiness. Seeing her panic rise, I said, "I'm right here with you, Rebecca. Can you feel me with you?" She immediately nodded yes, so I knew our connection could hold this much intensity. As long as she could feel the connection, we could go ahead and be with this child. I asked if she was seeing or hearing anything inside, and she shook her head no. "That's okay. Your belly is telling us the story we need to hear." Tears came and then sobs. I continued to stay with her, placing my hand on my own belly in empathy with her, talking softly sometimes, leaning in. As her system began to calm, she put out her hand and asked me to take it. I did, and that additional reassurance seemed to further cement the connection between me and what I believed must be a very small child within her.

When she opened her eyes, she said very softly, "I'm not sure what that was about, but I felt very small and very lost and very alone. Sometimes almost like I was coming apart and would disappear." We talked about what it must have been like to have parents who were losing a child to cancer right when she needed them most. "No one's fault at all, and yet for the baby you were, the loss must have felt intolerable." We sat quietly with that for a while. Then she nodded yes.

All these years, her body had been holding on to these early experiences. Because we need to feel connected to our parents or caregivers when we are small and Rebecca's parents didn't have the wherewithal to be attentive to her, an implicit knowing had grown in her that people leave. As a result, her neuroception was always scanning for signs that someone important to her might suddenly go away. This left her to live her life right at the edge of panic. Now, with two people not showing up for her, the panic had reached fever pitch. The pain of emotional neglect and abandonment has often been described as an experience of annihilation, living at the edge of a black hole where—in an instant—one might fall into an endless abyss. We are so in need of one another—of warm eyes looking back at us, of arms poised to hug us when we most need skin-to-skin contact—that this quiet kind of excruciating developmental trauma Rebecca was reexperiencing may well be the most painful and damaging of all, often leading to pockets of disorganization like those coming to her now.

Because of Rebecca's courage, we were able to do the slow but important work of building a foundation of security inside her. She began to understand that—even if it is painful, and it most certainly was for her—her body was sharing the truth with her, and this was opening the door to healing. It took time and trust, but we held these powerful sensations together in many sessions, also taking time to rest together so her budding neural circuitry had time and support to fully absorb the healing experience and settle.

One day, a few months into our work, we were sitting quietly together and I asked her what was available to us on this particular day. Rebecca's eyes popped open and she said with surprise, "My whole chest feels warm!"

"Let's follow that!" I said with a chuckle.

We found ourselves breathing a little more deeply, waiting, listening to see what would happen next. "I see me and my aunt Lucy!" she said.

"Is there more to tell me?"

"We're just walking hand in hand in her garden. She's telling me a story, I think, and then scooping me up into her arms." As she spoke, a single tear was slowly making its way down her cheek toward her gentle smile.

"No wonder your chest feels so warm," I said. It felt so lovely to have this tender inner anchor make her appearance right in the midst of all this hard work. The little girl in the memory appeared to be about two or three years old, with the family likely still in the thrall of her sister's death. I felt so grateful for this sanctuary for tiny Rebecca.

Over the months ahead, as we moved through so many memories of need and panic, loss and abandonment, we were also offered memories like this one of walking with her aunt Lucy. Some of these emerging experiences came from later in Rebecca's childhood when her parents were recovered enough to fully delight in her. All of her experience was gradually integrating into the whole story of her life. Meanwhile, back at work she still didn't like it when her boss was cranky or absent, but she had more room for the reasons in his own life that might be at play and—most important—the inner resources she needed to nourish her as she went through interpersonal challenges. Things were more complicated with her boyfriend, who seemed to be at his own implicit crossroads. I referred them to a couples therapist I knew would be able to help them sit with their Little Mes until they had the resolution that their relationship needed.

MEETING LITTLE ME

Years of doing this healing work with my clients has taught me that there is an inner wisdom that guides the process, an inherent movement toward healing that knows the way, once we have the support we need. Many years ago, a friend of mine who was in therapy told me that her therapist noticed that she was working very hard to unearth the little one inside of herself. With all the compassion in the world, he said to her, "You can just put down that pick and shovel, sit back, and listen for the whispers in your body. They are announcing the arrival of the one you are yearning to meet." She said that even though old implicit patterns sometimes required her to pick up her digging tools again, his words made all the difference. Over time, as her trust in him and in the process grew, that kind of relaxed opening to sensations and images became second nature. Although I would encourage you to seek out a therapist if you are struggling with a great deal of emotional pain, I will also just say here that much of this work is also possible with the right listening partner or partners. In the meantime, I'm also right here with you guiding the way. Let's begin by gathering some supplies:

- Your journal and a favorite pen or pencil.

- If your journal has lines, it would be good to also have blank paper for drawing, along with crayons or pastels—or whatever you prefer.

- Is there someone you want to invite to co-anchor this process with you?

Taking some first gentle steps, *gather up some photos* from your early life. They may be of you alone or include family and friends. Go through them slowly, noticing which ones feel particularly powerful to you. Some may bring smiles and warmth. Others may activate sadness or anger or some kind of undefined discomfort. Set them aside for further reflection. If there is one that brings especially warm feelings toward this child, you may want to set it on your nightstand or any place you will see this version of your young self regularly. Often, just returning frequently to focus on your Little Me can feel reassuring, especially if your parents struggled to provide the consistency and safety you craved as a child.

Another place to begin might be *conversations with parents and/or siblings* about your early days. Of course, it depends a lot on what kind of relationship you have with them now, but when and if you see an opening to do this, many people tell me that they have heard things they never knew that helped them in their healing journey. For instance, I worked with a young man for many years, and we were both often bewildered as to why he was so terrified of getting into intimate relationships. During a visit to his grandmother, she gave him an especially strong hug and very quietly said, "We didn't know if you would live through your first year, dear. I'm so glad you made it." He had no idea what she was talking about, so asked her to say more. "Well, your mother was so terribly depressed, she sometimes didn't even change your diaper all day—and your dad had to spend long, long days at work and was rarely home. She wouldn't let any of us help, either. Your first eighteen months were terrible. I wish I'd been pushier." His grandmother told him that his mother had emerged from that depression when he was about two years old. As a result, he had no explicit memory of the earlier time, and it was a forbidden subject in the family. Thanks to his grandmother, we could begin to sense how this profound abandonment early in his life had created terror of getting close and vulnerable with anyone.

If you decide to have some conversations with family, how you approach them matters, too. If your first impulse is to place blame, this is natural and understandable, especially if you suffered abuse or neglect as a child. However, if the day comes when you find yourself *moving from blame to curiosity*, you may be ready to just ask the questions you want to ask and to listen. Sometimes our experiences with family change over the years, as happened for Rebecca, so there is more closeness and understanding than when times were so painful. Some family members may feel more accessible than others. As each of us moves along in our healing process, it may become easier to keep in mind that each person has their own history and own implicit world that was guiding the way they related to us as children. When we approach them with this in mind and with an open heart, a safe space can open that may encourage deeper sharing. As you are listening to what they have to offer, your body may respond to the stories. A tightened belly, a warm chest, tensed or relaxed muscles. Breathing just a little more deeply can help you settle a bit. And journaling or sharing with your listening partner afterward will always strengthen the experience.

UNCOVERING THE IMPLICIT MEMORIES THAT FORM OUR CORE BELIEFS

The way our parents see us and relate to us eventually generates beliefs about who we are, how we can expect others to treat us, and the nature of the world in general. These beliefs begin with a felt sense in the body in response to our interactions with those close to us. With repetition, we translate these sensations into words. Many of us repeat these statements about ourselves over and over in the back of our minds—"I'm unworthy" or "I'll never find love" or "Everything will be okay"—until they become the codes we live by. As we turn our attention to them now, they become arrows pointing us toward the sea of our implicit memories. Some of them offer foundational support and others can become the starting point for healing our developmental wounds.

Below is a sample of phrases we might say to ourselves in our minds. Some are supportive and others perpetuate a negative sense of self. It is certainly not an exhaustive list, but perhaps some of them may prompt your mind to spot one that has been swirling in your own unconscious. As you say each one slowly, listen to how your mind and body respond. For example, if I say, "I'm unlovable," my mind says that this isn't true about me (not anymore!), and my body has no noticeable response. If I say, "I must perform to be worthy," there is a pause inside and I can sense that some part of me believes that. Through the work I've done, my affirmative response to this statement has become fainter and fainter, but some of this core belief lingers. Now, when I notice this, I consider it without judgment and with *curiosity* about the part of me that is still holding on to this belief. Scanning my body from toes to top, I can feel my breath is shallower and my shoulders and neck tighten a bit in the presence of this thought. I thank this part of me for speaking to me through these sensations and say that I will return to be with her.

At the other end of the spectrum, you may find you resonate strongly with some of the supportive statements. Paying attention to your bodily responses when you say these phrases will help to strengthen the parts of you who provide sanctuary for you every day, even when you aren't consciously aware of them.

If some of the bodily responses you receive are fairly intense, just be with a few phrases at a time. Doing them with a listening co-anchor is the most complete way to provide support for both of you. And your journal, while not quite the same thing, can also be a receptive container. Feel free to pause after any of the phrases that resonate and make some notes.

- I find joy in little things.

- I disappoint people.

- I feel unsafe around people.

- I am not enough.

- Supportive people come my way easily.

- People would rather not be around me.

- I am unlovable.

- I am comfortable in my own skin.

- I must be a good child to be loved.

- I cause unhappiness for those around me.

- I am lovable even when I make mistakes.

- Something is wrong with me.

- I am unworthy.

- People are not trustworthy.

- I must perform to be lovable.

- When I'm scared, someone will help me.

- I am completely alone in this world.

- I have to take care of others and forget myself to be wanted.

- When the day is tough, I trust better days are coming.

While you are doing this exercise, other phrases may come up. It is so important to pause and attend to what your inner world is offering you. If these are the voices of suffering, they want to be heard and acknowledged as the first step toward relieving them of their pain and fear. If they are voices of joy and goodness, they are bringing you a gift.

After taking whatever time is right for you to do this exercise—be it hours, days, or weeks—there is a second part of this practice that will help us go deeper into Little Me's implicit world. This part invites you to be more contemplative, so set aside time and space—either alone or with a co-anchor—when you will be uninterrupted for a half hour or so. One very important part is for you to feel *accompanied* as you enter this tender world. One way is to bring me in by doing the practice through listening to my recording of it, which can also be found at jessicabaumlmhc.com/safe-meditations. Or if you prefer to do it in silence, you can listen first and then begin the practice. Or you and your co-anchor can guide each other through the practice, reading it step-by-step.

Now we're ready to begin.

- Going back to the wounding phrases that touched you, see if you can sense which one stands out the most for you. It may almost feel like it is calling you. This is what your Little Me believes to be true because of earlier unsafe experiences with attachment.

- Notice where in your body you feel a response to this statement. Check in with your full body—heart and belly, skin, shoulders, neck, jaws, breath, a sense of shakiness or exhaustion—whatever draws your attention. As best you can, notice these sensations without judgment and without trying to change anything—just receive what comes as valuable communication.

- As your body shows you where this belief is being held, gently bring your hand into contact with that area or, if you can't reach it, settle your mind and heart there. You are coming into a relationship with this younger part of you.

- Together, we will just stay there with any other inner or outer anchors you wish to invite.

- Take some little, deeper breaths here and just be with the sensation. As best you can in this moment, welcome what arises as a story of how hard it was for a younger part of you.

- Together, we can stay with the sensations that are coming up, as uncomfortable as they might feel, although it is also quite all right to pause if they become too intense. If we can hold this with the awareness that this is implicit memory, perhaps you will find compassion for your Little Me welling up. This younger you is sharing a long-kept secret with you right now. Yes, it was really that painful and scary, and you were alone with it at the time. Now these memories can finally be held with the care and tenderness that your Little Me had yearned for when the experience(s) occurred.

- Perhaps you can see your Little Me in your mind's eye. Maybe you notice how old they are, where they are in space and time. Perhaps this young one has a memory to share. All you need to do is listen and be their witness. A story might not come with every experience in your body because our earliest memories often consist only of sensations, without narrative. You can trust that your inner world knows how to bring your little one to you.

- As Little Me feels more and more known and accompanied, often the sensations begin to shift and soften. We can stay with this new experience of emerging ease. Soon you may feel a lessening of focus, signaling that it is time to return to outer awareness. Or perhaps the memory just begins to fade. Or perhaps you are getting tired and feel ready to stop for this day. You can let your inner world know that you want to come back to visit and offer more support. It will be possible to return and continue to build communication. As you are finishing for now, you might want to place a hand on your heart, expressing how special and deserving of love your Little Me is to you.

- You may also want to round out this practice by spending time with one of the phrases that is connected to a warm anchor inside. Repeating the phrase, sense what arises in your body and just rest there. It is such a good way to settle our bodies into the experience of goodness in us and the world.

- Each time you do this practice, it can be so helpful to journal and draw right afterward. Often our young ones express themselves more fully through drawing. Making time for this kind of expression invites your younger self to share more deeply about the origin of these strongly held beliefs. One practice I've found helpful is nondominant hand drawing. I'm right-handed, so I use my left hand because it helps me connect more fully to my emotions. Then I see what color pulls me. Rather than draw a picture, I just follow the energy in my body from being close to Little Me. Maybe that energy guides me to draw big circles or strong dark lines. It is another way for me to listen to her all-important story. There is more information about nondominant hand drawing in the Wisdom Notes.

Sometimes journaling that takes the form of free writing whatever comes to mind can help you access your Little Me's voice more readily. At other times, as you are just sitting quietly, you may hear single words that capture some aspect of the experiences that your young one shared with you in the practice—"loud" or "mean" or "towering over." You will be able to return to these words when you are ready to go into your Little Me's world again.

We're right in the heart of our work now, and this practice is something we will be doing many times as we offer sanctuary and healing to the Little Me who has been waiting for you for so long. The attention and care we are bringing to their embodied stories are the very disconfirming experiences we talked about in chapter 4—what we needed at the time of the wound but wasn't available to us then. As we offer a dependably safe and receptive relationship to our younger self, drawing in others whenever we can, we slowly mend what was ruptured in our hurtful past relationships.

HEALING YOUR ABANDONMENT WOUNDS

Almost all of our attachment wounds share one thing in common—a sense of having been abandoned by the people we needed the most. Our parents' childhood wounds are certainly a big part of the reason they can't offer us the kind of warmhearted acceptance and receptivity we need, but our cultural condition may be playing a large role these days as well. The pressures of what we are calling the hustle culture and the distractions of social media are so out of sync with our human need for slow, deep connection that we adapt by shifting into left-hemisphere functioning focused on tasks so as not to feel the pain. There is no relational circuitry on the left, only a profound aloneness.

When we're little, especially in the first two years of life, we are right-hemisphere creatures, constantly seeking the eyes and arms of people who really see us, who have the time and neurobiological readiness to respond with their right hemisphere's capacity for presence, contact, reflection, responsiveness, and delight—the ingredients of secure attachment we talked about in chapter 1. We want the settled feeling of being known, loved, and wanted. The truth is, most parents love their children and want the best for them, but it is also true that many aren't equipped to give us the experience of "feeling known." When we are met with something less than that, there is a starvation deeper than a lack of food. It is a form of abandonment that can be more keenly felt than just being left physically alone. The result of this left shift for so many families has been a well of emptiness inside every person living in what looks like a normal household. And it can be very confusing for our Little Me to feel so profoundly abandoned for no visible reason.

Jacob had come to therapy with me because he was bewildered, restless, and miserable. After we had settled in with each other for a few months, he said to me, "I haven't wanted to tell anyone this, but if I stop long enough to feel anything, I get this big hollow ache inside. Yet to look at my life, it seems like I have everything a person could want. And I'm not just talking about things, but people, too. Lots of friends, a partner who is good to me. I even have a dog who adores me. Am I just an unsatisfiable jerk?"

"Of course not," I replied. "I already know enough about how you grew up to have some sense of what it was like to be a child in that household." In another session, in a flat, fact-reporting voice, Jacob had told me that both his parents were high achievers and expected the same of their children. He said that he owed his success in the world to that. Because he grew up in an upper-middle-class home, all his needs were met. His parents rarely fought, and he had okay relationships with his brother and sister. There was a quality in his voice when he told me this story that woke something up in me. There was no aliveness. Just reporting. In one of our meetings, I asked him who had helped him with his homework.

"Sometimes Dad, sometimes Mom. Mostly no one, because I could figure it out for myself."

"Who did you go to when you were sad?"

"There was nothing to be sad about."

"What about if you got hurt?"

"That was frowned upon because I should have known better, but if I actually broke a bone, we went to the hospital."

At this point, my chest was aching for the child inside Jacob who'd had no one, and for the adult who was completely unaware of his loss. It wasn't going to help for me to speak about this now because he was going to have to experience it in his body to believe something traumatic had happened to him. I knew he was getting ready when he told me about the "big hollow ache inside." The safety that was growing between us was leading to trust and vulnerability. There was enough support for his right hemisphere—where the early wounding was stored—to begin sharing the sensations of his aloneness.

I have had my own experiences of encountering abandonment inside me. As trust grew in my therapy, my body brought the sensations of being a baby in my crib. I felt the cycles of terror and collapse as my autonomic nervous system moved from fear to hopelessness. My therapist Jo's steady care and wisdom offered enough support to be with such intensity. With some healing, I was also developing the capacity to witness Little Me rather than being completely swept up in her experience. This made room for the necessary deep grief for these early extreme losses. It is hard to find strong enough words for the anguish we endure when there is no one who is able to respond to our cries with comfort, no one who has the capacity to see and connect with the child we really are.

Abandonment can take many forms. Any parent whose own inner struggles make it challenging for them to create a safe and loving environment for their child will also have difficulty being fully present for their children. These unintentional lapses will cause inevitable ruptures. My friend Anna's mother, anxious because of her own childhood traumas, turned to her daughter for regulation, so Anna had to set her own needs aside in order to care for her mother. Another friend of mine, Dean, grew up with a critical father who himself had been humiliated by his own dad. Through no intention of his own, Dean's father filled his son with shame for any small "failures" in his attempt to be sure Dean succeeded. I have listened to hundreds of stories like these. Dean and Anna felt acute abandonment because their tender emotional lives were unseen by these well-meaning but hurting and hurtful parents.

Even when we love our parents, it's okay to have an awareness that how they related to us had an impact on us when we were kids.

Abandonment can take many forms.

Touching into the felt sense of what happened will help us build compassion for the parts of us that suffered. We can do this without blaming our parents. At the same time, one of our protective adaptations may be thoughts like "My parents did the best they could and loved me" or "Others had it way worse than I did." Both of these are true but can also be ways our system has protected us from the excruciating experiences of the abandonment we experienced.

As we are developing the capacity to listen deeply to our bodies, we can feel into our experience as very young children, and it is quite possible that we will sense that we had no concept that others had it worse. We also may realize that we had no knowledge of what our parents had endured. We simply yearned for connection, and, at times, no one was there. During this healing time, you may feel many deep emotions about what happened with your parents—anger, joy, grief, gratefulness, blame, shame. All of these feelings are real and important, and we can make room for them. One of the signs that healing is spiraling forward is when we have a balanced sense of what our little one experienced coupled with compassionate appreciation for the wounds of our parents, and the sweet connections that have also been passed down through the generations.

In the previous two practices, we focused on Little Me. Now, as we are coming toward the end of this chapter, we're going to spend some time with the quality of our early relationships. As we discussed in chapter 2, we internalize everyone with whom we've had emotionally meaningful relationships. In our early years, this means that the ones who raised us every day will have a very large internal presence in us. They continue to whisper—or shout—their messages to us every day, a force that awakens our body's patterns of activation and resulting behaviors. Even when this happens outside our conscious awareness, they have such a powerful influence.

A friend of mine since childhood said to me recently, "I try to make plans to do something new all the time, and yet I never actually do it. The other day, I had the opportunity to go to a painting class that was just about experimenting with color. Absolutely no chance that anyone would be critiquing my work. But when the time came to sign up, it felt like too much. If this was a one-off thing, I wouldn't pay any attention to it, but I just can't muster the energy to do things I believe would be wonderful."

We had spent a lot of time at her home when we were kids. Now, in my mind and heart, I began to see her as a little girl in a household with three loud, dominant older brothers, a critical father, and a mother who was so overwhelmed by the tasks associated with keeping her household running that she scarcely glanced at her daughter, who seemed so self-sufficient. No one in the family knew or cared what her interests were. I sometimes think that she probably learned before she was two that she was on her own. She had simply collapsed into a quiet obedience. When she expressed her doubts about attending this painting class, I could almost see five backs turned toward her and feel the energy of excitement draining away as it had many times in her young life. She still felt that there was little safe space for her to explore her creativity though she was now an adult and what she had lacked as a child seemed only a distant memory.

MOVING FROM THE SHADOW OF ABANDONMENT TO THE SANCTUARY OF SAFETY

These next two practices will help you get in touch with adult figures who were most influential in your early life and feel the qualities of these all-important relationships. As we have discovered, these people are still living inside of us through the process of internalization. Bonnie Badenoch calls them our "inner community" to honor their ongoing presence with us. Just as we carry our experiences of nourishment or wounding deep inside us, we also internalize theirs as we interact with them. As we slow down and embrace Little Me, this young one will guide us to those who have been most nourishing and most harmful so we can help these internalized ones find healing, too.

Let me give you an example. Because I've been doing this work for some time, when I settle inside myself, I can become aware of my relationship with my father. I not only feel the sensations Little Me experienced in his presence, but also begin to have a felt sense of the anguish in him that prompted him to cast me aside. I get in touch with Little Him. These inner ones we internalized yearn for healing just as we do. They are, in fact, part of us now. Even if on the outside these parents (and others) never heal, the part of them that lives within us can and will. That such profound resolution is possible is one of the greatest gifts of the wisdom inherent in our neurobiology.

This is long, deep work, but these two practices will help you open a door into your inner world, if only just a little crack right now. As you sense the depth of healing that is possible, you may find you want to work with a therapist who can hold this kind of exploration with nonjudgmental presence and warm care. It is also possible that, as listening partnerships deepen into profound trust, the two of you can care for the Little Me and others who inhabit your inner world.

EMBRACING YOUR LITTLE MES AND THEIR COMPANIONS

As you do the following practices, your sense of being accompanied as you move into this tender territory is very important. You can listen to the audio version of me speaking the following words at jessicabaumlmhc.com/safe-meditations, or you could invite a companion and read aloud to one another.

It is important to have some uninterrupted time to do this practice, so select a quiet place that feels safe and welcoming to you. Inside or outside, it doesn't matter. Find a place where you can sit or lie down. Just be wherever feels most comfortable. Bring your journal and drawing materials in case you want to respond to the practices with illustrations as well as words.

> It is a little challenging to write these practices because once we begin doing them, we want to follow what is unfolding naturally. It's as though there's a fork in the road after every piece of practice, so the next step may not be the same as what I've written exactly. It's always more important to follow what is wanting to happen inside than to go step-by-step. Wherever this practice takes us, you can always count on me holding your hand.

- We're going to begin with you standing outside the home where you lived when you were young, the first one you remember. Whatever age you are, I am standing by your side and taking your hand, if that is comfortable for you. I ask, "How would it be to go toward this home together?" I am just here to follow you and carefully listen to all you have to share.

- You might feel hesitant to approach your home. We can be with that. There is no hurry. You might boldly walk in the front door. We can be with that. All your feelings and responses are welcome. I am here to just be with you as the felt sense of the primary relationships in your early years gradually reveal themselves to us.

- If we do enter the home, I ask, "Who else is here?" Take your time feeling your way into this home. It could be that no one is here. We can be with that. It could be there are quite a few people here, and maybe someone greets you. We can be with that. Whenever sensations begin to come into your body, we'll pause together to sense which family member or situation is stimulating these feelings. We may begin to meet people who became inner anchors for you. We may also encounter people who feel frightening or absent or anxious. Whatever happens, we can be with that together.

· Depending on what happens here, I may also ask, "Where will you go in your home? And what happens with others in the family when you go there?"

· At some point, we may sense that a particular relationship is wanting additional attention. Perhaps your mother is in the kitchen cooking with her back turned to you, and she doesn't turn around to greet you though she knows you have arrived. Or your older brother runs past you but pauses for a second to give you a big smile. Something inside you lets you know that this is a place to pause. We can check in first with what sensations are waking up in your body through this encounter. As we comfort your Little Me, we can also keep some awareness of the other people around us in this house. As Little Me settles, we may feel ready to turn to one of these people and ask them about their inner experience in this moment. "Mom, what is hurting or scaring you that you stay turned away from me?" You might ask your sibling, "What are you feeling inside when you smile at me like that?" Sometimes an answer comes in the form of sensations that are clearly from the other person. Sometimes you might feel the other person's hesitation to share. And sometimes there is nothing at all. But even then, we have offered contact and more will come from that. Maybe not now, but it will come when the time and conditions are just right.

- With a sense of gratitude for whatever may have happened, you and I can either settle somewhere in the house or go back outside. Taking some little deeper breaths, we return to this present moment. Leaving some time for journaling or nondominant hand drawing can allow Little Me and the other person in the relationship a chance to share more deeply.

- As you conclude this practice, remember that you can return to this home a thousand times and always find some new delight or an experience with someone who was once and possibly still is close to you that needs healing.

The second way of approaching these inner relationships seeks to help us float back to our earliest days as infants and toddlers, re-awakening the sensations that formed our sense of ourselves, others, and the world before we could make explicit memories. Our experience in the womb, the nature of the dynamics between our primary caregivers, and the state of their nervous systems left lasting imprints on us that we can be open to now. Because we are used to thinking of memory as the stories we recall, accessing sensation-only memory can initially feel less true. My clients tell me that gradually, with repeated visits to these early times, a coherent sense of what early life was like for them begins to take shape. As always, accompaniment is the key to healing, so however you can be anchored—my voice, a listening partner, a therapist—is a gift to every part of you.

- Gazing at a picture or two or three of yourself as a baby can be a helpful place to start. Choose one that draws you in this particular moment. After spending some time with this infant, begin by closing your eyes, getting yourself into a comfortable position where you feel safe and held.

- Keeping this infant in mind and heart, gently call on the energy of a primary caregiver, whether it is your mother, your father, an older sibling, your grandparent, or an adoptive parent. You can ask, "What did it feel like to be in relationship with them?"

- Your body might begin recalling sensations or feelings connected to that experience. When we are babies, our bellies, hearts, skin, and muscles are so sensitive to those near us.

- If sensations come, let's gently and slowly place a hand wherever they are. Just be with the sensations with as little judgment as possible. Right now we are going to just receive them. It may be that you won't feel any sensations this time. Just your offer to be with this little one is a gesture of healing. You can trust that.

- If sensations do come, welcome them as best you can in this moment. We can recall that these are memories. We can trust the wisdom of this body to reveal whatever is needed for our healing.

- Let's spend a few more minutes here just feeling into the safety of this moment and giving permission for something to emerge if it is ready. Whatever happens is just right.

- When you sense it's time, slowly open your eyes, sending the message that you will be back for more listening to this language of early sensation. To translate embodied feelings into something visible, this is a perfect time to do some nondominant hand drawing. Just allow your crayons or pastels to flow across the page as your body directs. More than one image may emerge. Then, as you feel a sense of completion, hold some tender care around this experience, whatever it was, as you move into the rest of your day.

- If no outer anchor was with you during this practice, I encourage you to take whatever may have come up to someone you trust and to write about it in your journal. By having these experiences witnessed, we amplify the healing possibilities through accompaniment.

- On another day, you may want to focus on a different caregiver. Perhaps you might notice if they were less available, focused on tasks, anxious, scared, happy, loving, warm, or kind.

Both of these practices will help you begin to establish connections with your inner community. The nurturing ones you internalized will become stronger anchors with each contact, and the inner pairs that still carry pain and fear can be offered disconfirming experiences. As these healing moments of intergenerational resolution accumulate, you will feel more whole, more safe, and more secure within yourself.

When anxiety or other hard sensations do come up, it can help to remember that it's not about getting rid of these experiences. Many of us have been encouraged to fix these uncomfortable feelings, but this is not what our Little Me needs. These experiences integrate when we invite our Little Me to share fully. When they feel seen, known, and welcomed by us, just as they are, the old sensations, emotions, and core beliefs have what they need to shift toward the kind of secure relating we are creating for them. Abandonment is embraced by presence. Shame is met with acceptance. Fear finds safety. And unpredictability is steadied by the consistency of our nonjudgmental, loving care.

In the next chapter, we will explore how the wounds sustained by our Little Me can impact our current relationships. We'll discover why we might be continuing old patterns we witnessed and experienced when we were small. With this awareness comes the enormous opportunity that this work offers to help us heal our past wounds. We can begin to feel a sense of agency if we are in unsafe relationships, unhappy dynamics, or painful "trauma bonds," and understand that these complicated dynamics can also lead to a personal awakening and a sense of personal empowerment. With this new, deeper awareness of the multiple layers of embodied memory you have sifted through in your inner work and the support of a growing community of anchors, you can start moving away from these painful cycles. Although coming to understand that we attract others to us partly because of the implicit expectations that we carry can feel disappointing, if we look at it with the newfound wisdom and perspective we have gained, we can see the opportunity available to us now to foster a true sense of safety and wholeness inside that will lead to more meaningful and deeply satisfying relationships.

CHAPTER 6

HEALING THE PATTERNS THAT KEEP US STUCK

A longing for warm, safe relationships is built right into our DNA. No matter how many painful experiences we have had, this yearning never goes away. It is the thing that keeps hope alive and eventually may attract us to safe relationships that can hold and heal us. At the same time, our implicit world carries the embodied expectations of how relationships will be for us based on how they have been in the past. If our family home was chaotic, our bodies believe in the deepest way that close relationships will contain this same kind of upset. If our home was silent and sterile, this is how we unconsciously expect all relationships to be. If we were lucky enough to be raised in a warm, secure, safe home, making nourishing connections as adults may be mostly effortless.

There is so much going on when we feel a strong pull toward another person, be it a lover, a friend, a child, even a work relationship. The pheromones whose scent we recognize and the kind of physical attributes we prefer have their roles to play, but the long-term trajectory of a relationship is usually most influenced by the implicit expectations we carry in our bodies from earlier attachments. You may be sensing how the familiar has such a powerful draw for each of us. Like a hand beckoning us to go toward particular people, that allure can be so compelling.

Given that you were drawn to this book, it may be that your early attachment experience was disrupted by parents or others whose own wounds made it hard for them to offer you safety. Painful bonds like these leave us with twin pathways inside ourselves, and it can often be difficult to know which road to follow. On the one hand, we are driven by the strong need to find people who will fill the empty places inside of us, which leads our whole system to scan for people who can protect us from these aching wounds, many of which remain out of our conscious awareness. At the same time, we experience a powerful, visceral draw—what I like to call our "magic radar" because it happens outside of our conscious awareness—toward the fundamentally unsafe relational pain that is familiar to us. One of my clients said to me, "You could line up fifty people I don't know, and I would consistently be drawn toward the most alcoholic person in the group." She summed it up saying, "Instead of looking for a needle in a haystack, I magnetize the familiar needle out of the haystack." Our embodied anticipations, most often operating below our conscious awareness, really are that strong.

Emotionally intimate relationships often begin when we find

the one we believe will save us, and yet these relationships will often quickly descend into misery when each party's implicit wounds emerge and then converge with the other's. Old protective patterns come into play, and the initial sense of safety and love can drown in the unhealed wounds of both people. Often we can find ourselves caught in cycles that confirm each other's core beliefs. Both people are in constant pain—unable to find their way toward a different way of interacting. We often call these relationships *trauma bonds*, because both people are helplessly repeating the painful patterns of their early trauma. At the same time, both of them look toward the other person to fix their wound rather than turning inward and getting support to heal their own injuries. Looking toward the other to act differently and heal our inner pain can keep us trapped in the notion that if our partner could just show up differently, we would be fine. Many of us, myself included, have been trapped in periods of longing for an avoidant partner to finally show up emotionally. For me it took quite a bit of time to build the awareness that the deep feeling of missing my partner and longing for him was so very familiar to me because my Little Me had experienced that type of yearning for connection with an unavailable parent.

Because of all the work I have been doing both in therapy and with my own anchors and listening partners, I can look back at my past relationships with eyes of compassion. I can now see the childhood pain that each of these connections awakened in me. In this book, I have spoken at length about the relationship that set me on this deep course of inner healing. Now, when I look back on this connection, I realize how much our coming together felt like a dream. I remember loving the vibration of his voice over the phone during his frequent calls. His intense drive to be with me was palpable. He wanted me. Little Me felt an unfamiliar sense of safety in the constant shower of his intense desire. When we hugged for the first time, it felt like home. The home I had been waiting for since the losses of childhood.

Before I met him, my protectors had been taking care of me for a long time, keeping me from being in conscious contact with the pain and fear surrounding my childhood wounds of abandonment and chaos. He showed up as such a caring person and wanted to be helpful in any way he could. From the moment we connected, we were constantly on the phone. He showered me with romantic gestures and poetry. It felt so good. I recognize now that, in addition to the sincere love we felt for each other, we were also two hungry children trying to swallow each other up so we wouldn't feel the fear and pain that was always close by.

All my unhealed wounds were still bubbling underneath, so even with his constant attention, the intensity of my work life and the flow of anxiety in my nervous system continued. At the time, these actually added to our attraction. I know he admired how accomplished I was. He was impressed by my career and commented approvingly on how hard I worked. How much my anxious self needed him was also clear to him. He had shared that his father worked hard and was super accomplished, but often distant, while his mother suffered from anxiety and often pulled at her son to put aside his own needs to tend to the turbulence in her own world. Then again, she was also a warm and wonderful dreamer (like him). Looking back, I can really feel how our histories were intertwining as together we traveled the same old paths we had both followed when we were small. Sometimes there was nourishment, but other times only the stark reality of abandonment. In my inner world, I now carried not only a felt sense of my experience of my own parents, but I was also beginning to carry a felt sense of both his parents as well. At the same time, I believe we were also meeting and nourishing each other. I knew intuitively that I was gently touching wounded places inside him in ways that had been painfully neglected by his father.

Inside me, the little one who was receiving this ocean of love was standing next to the child who was still acutely feeling the certainty of abandonment, the core wound of my childhood. I was safe and not safe at the same time. Just a few months into our deepening connection, I remember standing in the parking lot of a hotel having a conversation with him. Being a couples therapist, I know how relationships tend to go, and also how much earlier life experience can begin to impact them. I said, "One day our wounds will come up. One day I will feel alone, and you might not feel so special. We will not always feel this high we are currently on. It's just the beginning of the relationship and there are a lot of euphoric neurochemicals floating around inside us." He listened but didn't really understand what I was trying to express. It turns out that the enormous release of dopamine (the neurochemical of seeking one another), serotonin (the chemical of contentment), norepinephrine (racing heart and sweaty palms), and oxytocin (the bonding chemical that increases loving trust) brought on by falling in love was making us somewhat blind to everything but this moment of intense feeling. In my conversation with him, my own terror of loss was causing me to step slightly outside this rapturous state to issue a warning, while he was completely swept away by this flood of chemicals, on cloud nine, and legitimately deaf to my concerns. He was convinced I was the person he should have been with his whole life. Even with my concerns about the future, I felt good agreeing with him.

Around our third and fourth year, I could feel him starting to pull away. I don't know what specific wounds were awakening in him, but something was activating his need for everything to be perfect. The inevitable good days and tough days that happen in all relationships felt intolerable to him. He began to work at all hours of the day and night, both to sedate his discomfort and to keep some distance from me. At that point in my life, a slight change in closeness woke up my Little Me's terror of being abandoned. Panic was rising in me as I couldn't find any way to help him or to pull him back to me. So I redeployed one of my most brilliant adaptive strategies: I worked harder for his love through self-sacrifice.

All of this made his protectors more frantic, too. At random times he would get drunk or cause a fight. Or he would act out in ways that were confusing for me—speeding, for example. Looking back, I see that he was attempting to blur the turmoil inside himself by living his life on the edge. Both my father and sister had behaved this way, frightening me many times, so those wounds were also waking up in me. With both of us caught in the swirl of our own implicit memories, the relationship no longer felt safe to either of us. He became more and more convinced that I didn't love him enough. He began to resent my work, the very thing he had loved about me in the beginning. Despite my urgent attempts to reassure him, nothing could touch the waves of implicit pain (and the convictions that came with his core wounds) that were overwhelming both of us. As we have discussed, when two people are both feeling afraid, with both of their nervous systems stuck in fear states, their systems adaptively focus on threats and this prevents them from getting back into connection. Instead, we stay in protection and repeat the cycles of childhood, moving further and further away from safety and healing.

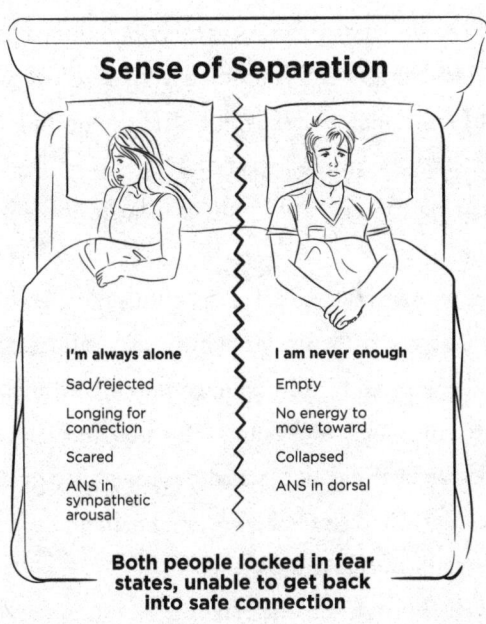

Sense of Separation

I'm always alone	I am never enough
Sad/rejected	Empty
Longing for connection	No energy to move toward
Scared	Collapsed
ANS in sympathetic arousal	ANS in dorsal

Both people locked in fear states, unable to get back into safe connection

It is so sad that the experiences that drew us together at first—our mutual craving for closeness and a shared admiration for each other's work—ended up being the very things that tore us apart when our wounds surfaced. We were more and more caught in the daily misery of a trauma bond, the repeating cycles of activating each other's core wounds and falling back into protection. The key change that helped me do what was necessary to break out of this cycle was beginning to be aware of the connection between my current anguish and my childhood wounds. I knew I had to break this pattern and get help. He could not choose to make that shift with me. As I slowed down and began the long journey of healing the childhood wounds inside me, I was able to get in touch with more and more of my early painful memories. I believe my increasing quietness as I underwent this process terrified him. He said, "I so much preferred being with you when you were overworked and anxious and I could help you!" A light bulb went on inside me. In his wounded state, he needed me to be like his mother so that his urgency in caring for me could protect him from his own pain of abandonment.

With great sorrow, I realized the connection was beyond repair, and I made the difficult decision to sever all ties. Lovingly, I told him, and I blocked him from all contact electronically in order to protect my emotional well-being. This necessary boundary gave me the space for healing, but it also deepened my grief, exposing me to a raw, intensified state of emotional pain and physical sensations that I wasn't anticipating.

Once I was through the initial pain, I began to see that perhaps my partner was meant to be in my life, as he became the biggest catalyst for my own healing. It was clear we had a very deep and intense love from the beginning. I do believe that part of it came from a healthy place. We were two genuinely caring human beings. And part of it was the attraction felt by two inner children whose need to be seen and cherished had never been met. It feels heartbreaking that relationships that start with such love so often don't work out because one person is ready to walk the path of healing and the other isn't.

With the support I was getting from my therapist and other anchors, my system could finally begin to be with the felt sense of my early abandonments. I had no idea how profound those losses had been. This sensitive state of awareness that I felt over the ending of this relationship brought me face-to-face with the ingrained hurt of my childhood. I remember days passing in which I felt like a small child alone in my apartment, faced with so much pain and fear, regressing at times, and not able to fully function as an adult. Simple daily tasks like checking the mail or grocery shopping became monumental efforts, as I was sometimes swallowed up in resurgent feelings of being completely alone. I was more and more clear that I was in the throes of deep longing for my partner while also understanding that these intense feelings had roots in the yearning and aloneness of my early life.

At times, with the support of others, I tried to just hold space for these explosive sensations. To this day, I am in awe at the profound capacity of our inner worlds to feel so acutely. I knew this was my window into what it felt like to be so young, but to experience it again in my body was surreal. I had periods of dissociation in which I felt separated from my own body. This distancing from sensation was trying to protect me from the full effect of the loss I was feeling.

Looking back on this experience, I am grateful for the perspective that meeting these tender younger parts of myself was both necessary and transformative. As deep as the pain was, I felt as if I was sewing back together the rough edges left by all the losses, and reconnecting with my fundamental faith in the power of nurturing relationships.

We come into relationships with one another not only for protection from our inner pain but also with the inner hope of healing. Had my partner also been able to recognize these childhood wounds for what they were as they surfaced, we might have been able to heal together. Sadly, it takes quite a bit of emotional healing and awareness to be able to both feel these old wounds rising up in us and recognize their origin at the same time. In the end, it was heartbreaking for me to realize that my partner was experiencing implicit memories of his earliest and deepest attachment fears and sensations but couldn't make this connection. He believed it was me who was causing him pain, while hurting him was the very last thing I ever wanted to do.

Our work in this chapter is to recognize how old wounds might be coming alive in our relationships now. In chapter 4, we worked on building interoception, and in chapter 5, we visited our early relationships with our Little Mes. Our work throughout this process will look more like a spiral than a straight line as we return again and again to all of these practices for deepening our connection with our inner world. Now we'll be adding some ways to get acquainted with the *relational patterns* that we see emerging over and over in our lives.

TRACING OUR RELATIONAL PATTERNS

As my own story reveals, old patterns can emerge in our relationships, often without either partner quite realizing it until it is too late. Relational patterns are often comprised of some combination of how we adapted to earlier relationships, how we saw others around us adapt, or what tendencies we have because of our temperament. Miranda, one of my clients, summed it up this way: "If I see someone looking helpless and in need, I forget myself entirely and rush toward them just as I did with my mother. But if someone pulls at me looking for affection, I back up and sometimes feel resentful like I did with my younger sister. And when things get overwhelming, you'll find me in a corner with a book. That comes from having to deal with all the chaos in our big family. I'm an introvert and I need quiet time. But I also watched my father vanish behind the work he brought home almost every evening. That hurt me, but I also learned to do it myself."

Miranda and I had been working together for a couple of years, and more and more she was developing what we can call a *caring observer*. When we are met with warm nonjudgmental care, our brains begin to develop a greater capacity to step back just a little bit and witness ourselves with more compassion. Miranda could both feel her experience and watch it with kindness at the same time. What a lovely gift we can give each other just by being truly present and listening deeply.

When Miranda first came in, she was bewildered about all the different and contradictory ways she responded to people. "Sometimes I rush in to save people and other times I just want them as far away from me as possible. What's up with that?" We talked about her wheel of attachment, and how the various relationships she had experienced created different feelings and protective responses in her. It is actually very rare for a person to have a single attachment style. In our healing work, Miranda began to feel how she had developed several attachment styles in response to the needs of the various people in her life. Because connection is a biological imperative, we are continually in a dance with those close to us that balances our yearning for contact with our other great need for safety. Miranda could stay close to her mother by giving herself up, while still protecting her own energies by pushing her clingy little sister away. She only discovered how intricately the two responses were connected when she realized that she had been so exhausted by meeting her mother's needs as a child that she didn't have anything left for her younger sibling. As we were with her younger self, her feelings of guilt about the way she treated her sister gave way to compassion for her exhausted self and for the suffering of everyone in the family.

All of us have this kind of complexity inside, and so as we do the following practice, I ask you to expect to encounter a great diversity of adaptive responses. Begin with as much warm curiosity and lack of judgment as you can while you invite your inner world to show you just how it was that you developed the patterns that arise in your relationships now.

Often, the intimacy of our romantic relationships provides a good place to begin this exploration, but it is also possible that an important friendship or parent/child connection may be most impactful for you. It is good to begin with whatever relationship your inner world offers. As we settle into this reflection, it will likely reveal persistent patterns that often echo your earliest experiences with attachment. You may discover recurring themes, such as feelings of inadequacy or fear of abandonment, which might reflect your most per-sistent implicit convictions about the way relationships are for you. Side by side with these revelations, you will likely also find healthy, supportive themes like a tendency to feel great tenderness toward children or a clear sense of when to say no. You can repeat this practice with anyone who comes to mind, at any time. Let's just take it slow and do our best to be open to what comes up spontaneously as we ex-tend a heartfelt invitation for those living in our inner world to share themselves with us.

- How we begin always matters. Find a safe and comfortable place where you won't be disturbed for the next half hour or so. Having a co-anchor with you is always helpful. You may want to gather up your journal and drawing supplies so you can take some time after this reflective practice to allow for more deepening and expansion of the experience.

- Invite your mind to scan through the adult relationships that have felt particularly meaningful for you. There is no need to hurry this part of the process. In fact, your first session with this practice may be doing just these two steps. Afterward, you could make note of the relationships that stood out for you. Or you may find that one particular relationship jumps out immediately, asking for attention. If you feel pulled to go further, go on to the next step.

- Many of our most profound relationships have a whole array of qualities, some of them that feel nourishing and some that contain enduring pain and fear. They will each be experienced differently in our bodies. As each particular memory comes to you, pause to check in with your muscles, belly, and heart. Notice how your breathing is affected (is it shallower? deeper?) and what happens to your level of activation (calmer? more agitated? losing focus?).

- Slowly be with the sensations that are coming up. It can be helpful to remind yourself that these bodily feelings may be the tipping point for an implicit memory to emerge, letting you know that a younger part of you is also being touched.

- Consider for a moment what in the scene is activating these sensations. Is it something being said to you? Is it an action, or a lack of something?

- Ask yourself, "Are there other times that my body has felt just like this?" Then pause and wait for whatever answer might arrive. You don't need to dig around inside for an answer or make up a story (something our left hemispheres will want to do). You can just wait as openly as possible.

- If a memory from earlier in life arrives, welcome this younger part of you and listen for the similarities in feeling between the memory from the current relationship and the past experience that is coming to you. The events being remembered may not be similar, but the emotions and the beliefs arising from the emotions are likely to be the same.

- If there is pain and fear in this memory, what did this younger part of you need at the time? If there was shame, acceptance is the antidote. If there is grief, comfort. If there is fear, sanctuary and safety. We can offer whatever was needed right now.

- For support, you could share this with the co-anchor who is with you or call to mind another trustworthy person. I would also be honored to accompany you by reading this practice to you or through remembering that we are together.

- You may feel drawn to make some notes in your journal or do some nondominant hand drawing.

- When you feel ready, see what additional memories come forward with this person. We can celebrate those moments that nourished us. With each embodied remembering, those inner anchors are strengthened. We can also be open to those experiences that harmed us. Each time we witness and care for those parts of us who hold pain and fear, something heals and we become more settled inside. When others accompany us, we internalize their care and add to the sanctuary of safety that our inner world is becoming.

Along with the practices from chapters 4 and 5, this one can become a daily reflection for us throughout our lives. By regularly spending time with our current relationships and allowing them to guide us back to unhealed child wounds, we can get in touch with what Little Me is seeking to resolve in our adult relationships. Our relational challenges begin to make sense to us, and our own caring observer, who can provide witness and care for our inner ones, grows stronger. If your wounds come from when you were really young, it is particularly important to do this practice in the presence of an anchor, therapist, or coach. Again, the younger the wound, the more adult anchoring we need to heal it.

As you do this practice with a few different people who have been important in your adult life, you will likely begin to notice the repeating themes and attachment wounds that are coming up. As I spent time visiting with my own Little Me, I felt the repeated presence of "I will always be left." It was there in every relationship, either in the background or playing a prominent role in how I was relating now. But the shades of it were different depending on the person in my life I was focusing on in the practice. I could feel in my body how my mother's preoccupation with work affected me differently from my father's disappearance into drugs.

> The younger the wound, the more adult anchoring we need to heal it.

As I stayed with these reflections, I also began to notice how the wounds generated some repeated adaptive responses that intended to protect me from contact with my childhood wounds. I would do everything in my power to please and stay in connection with the person so I wouldn't feel the overwhelming anxiety generated by my mother's absorption in her own life or the collapse into hopelessness and despair in response to the black hole of my father's abandonment.

I noticed that it was often easy to stay in connection in the early stages of coming together, but as the relationship mellowed over time and our attention was less focused only on each other, my terror increased along with my desperate attempts to keep this person close. This would increasingly touch my partner's wounds until we lost touch with each other entirely. It would have felt almost natural to feel critical toward myself for this pattern, but the tender care I received from my therapist and other trusted anchors combined with my growing understanding of the roots of this cycle of pain allowed my compassion for myself to grow and encouraged me to continue along the healing path that could change these tendencies.

Bringing my pain and loneliness to people who had proved they had the capacity to stay with me began to shift my belief from "people always leave" to "some people have a tremendous capacity to be present with me in my pain—no matter what." Over time, I came to truly feel and understand that not all people leave, and I began to draw in more available people to show up for me in my life. My neuroception was shifting from anticipating danger to *making room for the possibility of safety in relationships*. This deep inner change meant I had a better ability to find situations that could provide trustworthy connections rather than gravitating toward those people whose adaptation to stress and trauma was to leave.

THE WHEEL OF ATTACHMENT

Let's return to the wheel of attachment to explore the various ways people sustain attachment wounds. Then we can look at some of the ways they adapt in their current relationships to protect themselves from awakening the pain from early experiences with their parents and others. You may begin to recognize some of your own patterns along the way and want to pause to make some notes in your journal or to share with one of your anchors.

THE WHEEL OF ATTACHMENT

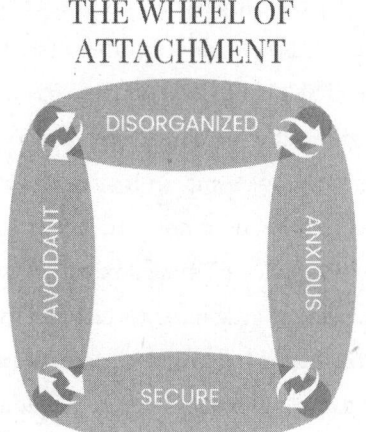

Spending some time with the diagram, we can begin to feel the flow between the attachment styles. Beginning at the bottom where security is solid, this consistent connection can become blended with anxious or avoidant attachment at the corners. At that point, there's still mostly security, but there are also some situations in which a parent either slips into agitated dysregulation or pulls away into left-hemisphere disconnection. As we continue up either side, the relative amount of anxiety or avoidance increases. Then as we reach the upper corners, fear escalates through increasing neglect and humiliation (on the left) or terror and violence (on the right). The child in this environment has no one to orient to and falls into agonizing disorganization.

Within a single household, it is possible a child will have significant experiences with each kind of attachment. When Randy and I first started meeting, we talked about his family. "I only remember four things about my father. He died when I was five. He would sometimes yell at my older brother, and that really scared me. He would go into his office after dinner, close the door, and then no one was allowed to go in—even if I stood at the door and cried. And he would snuggle me on his lap and read me stories. I really miss him sometimes, even now." In less than a minute, Randy had described the unpredictability of anxious attachment, the quiet abandonment of avoidant attachment, the tender warmth of secure attachment, and the trauma of losing his father at such a young age.

We went on to talk about his mother. "Mom was a different story. She was quieter than dad and seemed scared a lot of the time. When we got older, she told me and my brother about the violence she had experienced growing up. Her father drank a lot and on weekend nights would often beat up her mother. She said there were times she thought he might kill her. She and her younger sister were taken away when my mother was about seven and lived with their maternal grandparents after that. They were pretty old and not very interested in kids, so she was really lonely, but spent a lot of time making sure her kid sister was okay. It was hard to hear, but it explained a lot.

"After our father died, we learned to be quiet and obedient because Mom was so easily upset. She eventually remarried, but not until we were in college, so we were her guardians for a long time." My heart went out to Randy as I could feel the effects on him of the violence his mom had endured. Her system was carrying a lot of post-traumatic disorganization which the two brothers had felt and internalized. She had needed them to soothe her at the expense of their own full development.

With just these two parents, Randy had experienced every quadrant on the wheel of attachment. And we hadn't even begun to talk about his relationship with his brother. They were close, but Jackson was also often irritated and defensive with Randy. When his brother got mad, Randy could feel himself get scared and shut down, and this is what had gotten him into therapy. "I want to be able to be at ease with Jackson, and to not close up inside when he's irritable," he told me. "Instead, we feel so much tension around each other. Ironically, our wives are more comfortable with each other than we are."

The more often a particular kind of relational interaction happens, the more deeply ingrained the implicit expectation becomes in us. This then brings on the need to develop adaptations to either bring the parent closer or protect the child from being hurt again. They become so embedded in our inner world that they carry over into our adult interactions. I suggested to Randy that perhaps the way to closeness with Jackson was to explore the ways Randy had learned to protect himself when he was younger. We could just as easily have gone toward uncomfortable moments with his brother as our starting place, but Randy had told me that he was dreaming about being with his childhood family a lot, almost as though he was being called home. It seemed important to pay attention to that call.

Rather than turn this into a left-hemisphere exercise, we began to touch into the moments in his life with each parent that came most easily into his body. For his relationship with Jackson to change, his wounded implicit world would need to be soaked in the warmth and safety that was so often missing when the two brothers were younger. The first memory that offered itself was seeing his mother's anxious face and feeling every muscle in his body become tense. He felt himself to be elementary school age. Coming closer to this boy, Randy felt his belly tighten, too, as his breathing sped up. He heard the words, "I have to be good. I have to be good. I have to be good," as he moved toward her and leaned against her. This seemed to calm her down. And he relaxed.

Similar memories came up for our next few sessions, and each time, we listened and more deeply felt the wisdom of young Randy's response. As his mother calmed, she was more able to turn toward him and be present. He could feel how his body did just the same thing when Jackson was irritated with him. He had come to believe that the path toward closeness was to sacrifice his own needs to soothe the other person. Randy began to see how this played out in other relationships as well. But the most important part of our work was to be in relationship with his younger self until he could begin to feel that he had a sanctuary of support with us. No matter what his mood or actions, we would be with him, delight in him, welcome him. His whole body began to loosen up as his breath deepened and his joy came forward. The need to suppress himself diminished and just about disappeared. Over the months of this process, he said he began to feel brave with Jackson, who expressed surprise and also happiness at the change in him.

One day in the midst of this work, Randy said, "It's weird, but I also find I do the exact opposite thing sometimes. Instead of trying to soothe someone, I simply freeze them out. It's like a switch goes off in me and I turn my back." He paused, and then I could almost see the light bulb go on above his head. "That's just what my father did!" And we were off down another path in his interior world to explore how this way of protection had helped him. Along the way, he heard these words: "If they don't get close to me, they can't hurt me."

There are three parts of our response to our original painful or frightening attachment experiences. There is the *wound* that generates *adaptive, wise protective responses* in us that eventually become *beliefs* about ourselves and the way the world works for us. These then guide our responses in all our relationships. Often we hold contradictory beliefs within ourselves, each held by a different part of us. Randy had a part that learned to pacify others and a part that learned to simply shut the door. These two came out in different contexts with different people, but also sometimes with the same person under different circumstances. He recognized that his wife and children experienced both kinds of protective responses from him, leaving all of them unsure about how he would react.

"No wonder they get anxious around me!" he said. "All I'm doing is passing along the same upsetting experiences I had as a kid."

"Well," I said, "that's not all you're doing. You're also passing along the warmth and love you felt with both your parents. And now you're doing the necessary work to heal the wounds that have come down through generations in your family. That is something to celebrate."

Let's now spend a little time with the felt sense of each of the attachment patterns, and some of the ways protections and beliefs might form around each of them. These will just be examples to stimulate your curiosity about how it was for you. Each of us have completely unique experiences of attachment both nurturing and wounding.

THE TIGHTROPE WALK OF ANXIOUS ATTACHMENT

Unpredictability is the core feeling that generates anxious attachment. The parent bringing this experience is called *preoccupied* because their own inner world is sometimes flooded with their unhealed implicit experiences, but only sometimes. When this happens, it keeps them from being present with their child in those moments. Looking at the wheel of attachment, down near the lower right corner, the parent is offering security a good deal of the time, but is sometimes swept away. As we move up the right side of the wheel, there are more times the parent is lost to us, and by the upper right-hand corner, we are approaching disorganization because the parent is rarely able to offer safety and warm nonjudgmental presence.

One of my clients said she felt like her mother was always sliding between the lower right and the upper right, and that's what made her feel so anxious as a child. She never knew which mother would appear, the one she could count on to be a safe haven or the one who didn't see her at all because she was lost in her own world.

For those of us who have experienced this kind of unpredict-

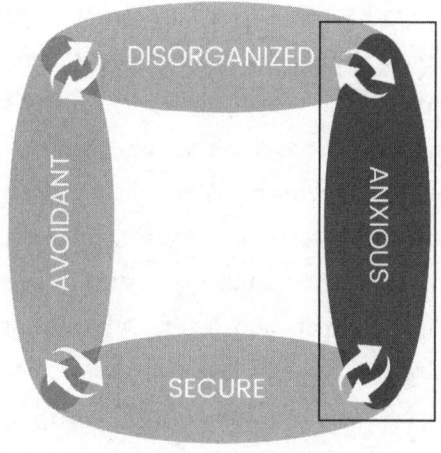

ability, the most common protection we develop is a desperate need for others to stay close so that the awful ache of abandonment doesn't wake up inside. The other person provides a living shield as long as their attention is laser-focused on us. This is often most intense in our romantic relationships. The initial stages of these relationships, where the pursuit of another is often mistaken for love, can be exhilarating. Fast, fast, fast goes the anxious love. While those with a secure attachment style may approach new relationships with a trusting heart, those of us who are anxiously attached wait in fear for the other shoe to drop. Is this too good to be true? We often need a lot of reassurance and co-

> Until the abandonment wound is healed, we tend to be drawn to what is familiar.

regulation from our partners, so the old pain of uncertainty and loss doesn't break through. Sadly, until the abandonment wound is healed, we tend to be drawn to what is familiar, partners whose wounds cause them to disappear when we need them the most.

If we are anxiously attached people, our nervous systems are in a near-constant state of hyperarousal, always on the lookout for signs of potential abandonment. When there is the natural easing of the initial intensity in a relationship, we feel threat. This hyper-vigilance can manifest in various ways, such as becoming overly dependent on our partners and fearing any time spent apart or needing verbal affirmations of love and commitment. We might struggle setting healthy boundaries, often prioritizing our partner's needs over our own. Sometimes we might tend to overanalyze words and actions, jumping to the worst-case scenario, fueled by the fear of losing our partner. These needs and behaviors, of course, have an effect on our loved one. If this partner is still feeling close, the fear doesn't make sense and can lead to despair when we can't be reassured no matter what they say or do. If our partner is frightened by relationship, they may enter their own protective state and pull further away.

As we've moved through our lives, these experiences have also generated some core beliefs. Here are a few that are particularly associated with anxious attachment. The list is anything but exhaustive. While reading this list, you may find yourself immediately hearing some of your own. "If I'm good, they stay." This one is often accompanied by "What did I do wrong?" when the other person leaves. "I have to know what they need before they do." "No matter what I do, it's never enough." After several relationships end painfully, "I am just no good in relationships." "I am unlovable." "I give up."

Pause for Reflection

Let's take some time to be with your experiences of anxious attachment as a child and as an adult, and of being around others whose anxiety impacted you.

- During childhood, in which relationships was there a sense of unpredictability, a wondering if a parent (or someone else close) would be able to attend to you in a way that felt settling?

- How does that inability to settle into safety and security feel in your body? Which relationships in your adult world have had a similar flavor?

- As you look around your world both past and present, who do you notice being sometimes present and sometimes not?

- Who feels anxious to you and how does that affect your body?

- What kinds of protectors have you developed to guard you from feeling the pain and fear of implicit memories that you carry from your experiences with anxious attachment?

- What core beliefs do you carry that arise from being in or around relationships that have anxiety as their primary component?

You may feel you want to take some notes about what arises with each question. Being able to go back and reflect on these with a trusted companion will help you get more deeply in touch with these inner relationships. We're just beginning this exploration, so we can go gently and slowly. Welcome whoever comes as best you can, trusting that your inner world will bring forward whatever you need to heal.

THE ACHING EMPTINESS OF AVOIDANT ATTACHMENT

The word most often spoken by those who get in touch with their experience of avoidant attachment is *annihilation*. When we are small, what we need most from parents (and other people we are meant to be close to) for those first two years are warm eyes offering presence because their own inner world is having a neuroception of safety. We need their emotional responsiveness that reflects our goodness and welcomes us wholeheartedly just as we are. When things get off track, as they do for all of us, we need them to be able to offer repair and reconnection. They can provide this if they have a healthy connection to their right hemispheres, because that's where the neural circuitry of warm attachment resides.

The more parents get trapped in their left hemispheres, the less they are able to offer this essential kind of emotional closeness to their children. In the lower left corner of the wheel of attachment, the parent will often be present but slip away into tasks-and-behavior-only land at times. The farther up the left side of the wheel, the greater the detachment from their child's emotional life until we get near the upper-left corner where all that remains is hatred, contempt, and a turned back. This is right at the edge of disorganized attachment.

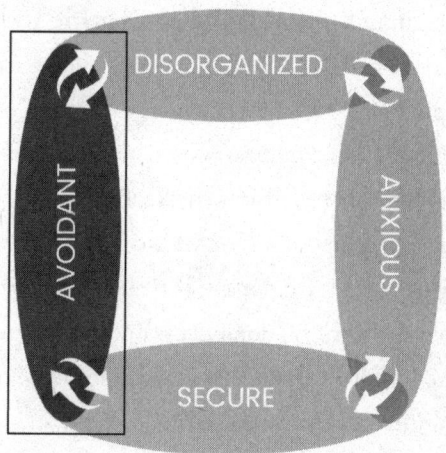

We are culturally struggling with more and more of this kind of attachment. The left-hemisphere values of good behavior, success, competition, and tasks being more important than relationships puts tremendous pressure on parents to prepare their children for this world. Unfortunately, this means our young ones are often left alone with their feelings. Because these parents aren't in touch with their relational brain, when their child comes and says, "I'm sad," the parent may look bewildered or ignore the child or deny the feeling or even get angry. To be unmet like this feels to the child like staring into an agonizing black hole of nonexistence. That can sound extreme, but this is what many clients have said to me. One of my clients told me, "When my mother looks blank when I tell her I'm scared, I feel as though I disappear in the most terrifying way. I can't even quite tell if I still have a body."

Parents who are locked in their left hemispheres are called *dismissing* because they simply do not have the neural circuitry to connect with those around them. Children who live with dismissive parents have the monumental task of developing protections to keep the aching emptiness at bay. Because our brains develop in tandem with our parents', the most natural protection is to also become isolated in our left hemispheres. This is so effective because we lose contact with the sensations in our bodies when we are disconnected from our right hemispheres, so we don't feel the acute emptiness. Nonetheless, this wound of annihilation lingers underneath, requiring certain kinds of protective behavior, especially in intimate relationships.

It is profoundly sad that consistent closeness and vulnerability become the enemy because they threaten to bring this person close to their inner wounds, exposing them to the intolerable pain of annihilation. At the same time, the inherent yearning for warmth and connection is still there, too. The emotional aliveness and desire for connection of someone who has an anxious attachment can feel attractive and hopeful to some avoidantly attached people. It touches their hope for warmth and closeness. The anxiously attached person can also be attracted to an avoidant person by the sense of left-hemisphere stability as a refuge from the chaos of their implicitly wounded parents.

As they first come together, they fall into an illusion of safety. As the relationship deepens, bringing vulnerability with it, the profound hole of abandonment threatens to awaken, and the avoidant one needs to pull away for safety. They may become angry, critical, preoccupied with work, or fall into addiction—anything to keep the intolerable feelings away. The greater the need to pull away, the more fear arises in the anxious one, who may then begin to need more contact and reassurance.

Inside the avoidant person, responding to these pleas for additional closeness feels potentially death threatening, as they face an emptiness that one client described as falling into an infinite abyss. But because of their protective distance from their own inner world, it all remains out of conscious awareness. As we are discovering, out of awareness doesn't mean that what's underneath isn't influencing whatever we do next, so the avoidant person backs away from the relationship, perhaps finds lots of left-hemisphere reasons why this isn't the relationship for them, and goes back to work.

It could be that not many avoidant people will be moved to pick up this book, but it is also true that most of us have some avoidant tendencies, like Miranda with her kid sister or Randy when he was overwhelmed. It is also likely that we've encountered left-shifted people in many areas of our lives and felt the effects of their protective cutoff from emotional connection. With the kind of pressures teachers face, all of us have likely had some left-shifted teachers who demanded performance but seemed to have little interest in what is happening with individual students. We may experience the same thing in our work lives.

What kinds of core beliefs might develop within a left-shifted person? Not surprisingly, many of them are judgments about other people rather than reflections on their own inner experience. "People are generally incompetent." "All people do is complain." "Pull yourself up by your bootstraps." "I respect grit and hard work." In a relationship that is starting to get close: "This person doesn't measure up to my standard for my life partner." "This person is too needy." "I am better off alone."

A Practice for Exploring Your Experiences with Avoidant People in Your Life

It will be helpful for us to touch in with our own experiences of avoidant attachment as children and as adults, and of being around others whose lack of emotional awareness and connection impacted us.

- During childhood, in which relationships was there a sense of having your emotional experiences dismissed?

- How does that lack of reflection and presence feel in your body? Which relationships in your adult world have had a similar flavor?

- As you look around your world both past and present, who are the people who seem left-shifted, task-oriented, and unaware of others' emotional life?

- Who feels emotionally empty to you, and how does that affect your body?

- What kinds of protectors try to keep you safe from feeling the pain and fear of implicit memories that linger from experiences of avoidant attachment in childhood?

- What core beliefs do you carry that arise from being in or around relationships that have emotional blindness and disconnection as their primary components?

Turning to your journal again to take some notes as you pause with each of these questions can help you slow down and listen more deeply. You may find that your world included more of one kind of attachment than another, or you may have had two parents with very different attachment styles.

Our present experiences will touch on these wounded, anxious, and empty places within us, but because we have been attending to them, we will more and more recognize their origins and be able to hold them tenderly with the help of our co-anchors, therapist, or trusted friends. For now, we are just slowly exploring this territory, and bit by bit developing our caring observer, who can help us spot the origin of these big feelings when they arise.

NOWHERE TO TURN: DISORGANIZED ATTACHMENT

With anxious attachment, we can usually find a way to connect with the upset person, often by soothing and regulating them, although this sometimes means we must abandon ourselves. With avoidant attachment, we can join them in the left hemisphere for some sense of togetherness. Both of these come at a cost, but we aren't completely alone and without resources for connection. As we are presented with experiences at the two top corners of the wheel of attachment—hatred and extreme emotional neglect to the left and chaos and violence to the right—we find ourselves in circumstances where our parents (or other close ones) are so internally disorganized that there is nowhere for us to orient ourselves and find relief. "Terror" is the word I hear most when my clients touch into this territory.

Because of the magnitude of the inner disruption and lack of safety that inhabits our bodies when we inwardly encounter experiences that have disorganized us, we are going to just gently be with

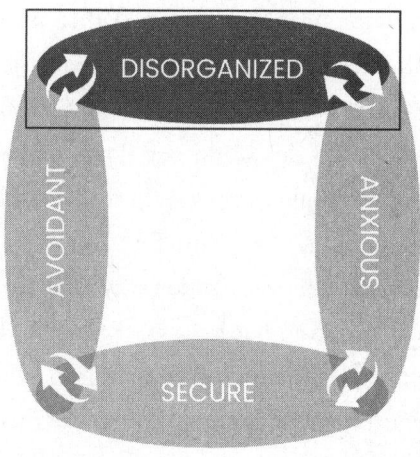

some understanding of this kind of attachment. It is likely that all of us have small pockets of disorganization from a time no one was available to us when we were terrified. Perhaps we had a nightmare and were even too afraid to get out of bed to get help. Perhaps we witnessed something horrendous and never shared it with our parents. Perhaps our parents inadvertently forgot to pick us up at school and we were left alone, frantic with fear that they wouldn't return. These are small moments that leave little pockets of terror inside. Unless something happens in our adult life to awaken these memories, they may never come to the surface and aren't strong enough to influence our day-to-day quality of life.

However, if our lives included hatred, extreme ignoring, and violence, it is essential that we be accompanied on the healing pathway, partly because of the intensity of the bodily sensations and emotions that hold these experiences. But the main need for accompaniment is because the core of the wound is having absolutely no one to turn to for any kind of safety. When my clients fall into disorganization, they need my voice and my calm, loving eyes as an anchor and resource for them to orient to as we find our way to safety together. We do this work very slowly. As we gently touch into these embodied implicit memories, we make time to rest a moment here and there before we move forward.

Big experiences of disorganization may come from being caught in war or natural disaster, but most of them come as intergenerational legacies, helplessly passed down from parent to child. Because our parents organize our brains to be like theirs, a mother or father whose childhood inheritance was chaotic disorganization has nothing else to offer their children. It is tragic. And it needs and deserves abundant holding from another.

Pause for Reflection

This is a good time to check in with your body and heart. If you have been feeling something stirring while you were reading this last section, it is important to acknowledge that some part of you has been touched inside. In this moment, writing about it in your journal, doing some nondominant hand drawing, or sharing with your listening partner or trusted anchor can provide witness and help settle the disturbance. Please be kind and gentle with yourself and make room for finding a therapist to accompany you throughout this passage.

What may also help is the next practice we're going to do.

SETTLING INTO THE ARMS OF
SECURE ATTACHMENT

There are also moments in our implicit history that can become the foundation for ongoing hope and goodness in our lives. Recalling them brings such a sense of settling and contentment to our muscles, bellies, and hearts, and a sweet, natural rhythm to our breath. These are the experiences from which we need no protection and out of which come nourishing core beliefs about who we are and what we can expect from the world. "I'm okay even when I'm messy." "Somehow, there's always enough help when I need it." "Kindness is so much more important than money." "I am loved."

As we begin to open ourselves to experiences of security, it is important to remember that parents are complex creatures, so the

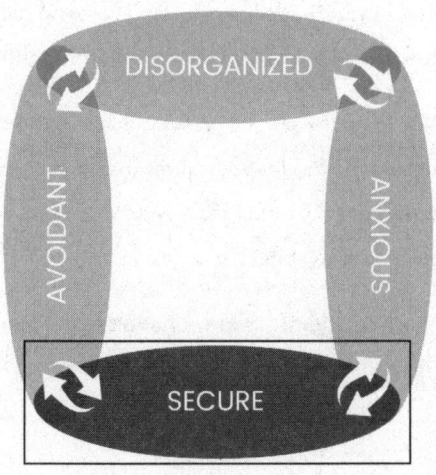

same person who was perhaps sometimes avoidant or anxious may also have offered many experiences of safe warmth, presence, and care. That is what life is like at the lower left and right corners of our wheel of attachment.

Pause for Reflection

Let's linger here as we invite these nourishing experiences to come alive within us.

- During childhood, which moments in your most significant relationships felt like sanctuaries of safety?

- How does your body respond to remembering these times? Can you just be with these nurturing feelings for a while?

- Who in your early life did you laugh and play with? How does your body feel remembering those times?

- Who in your early life was good at repairing ruptures? What happens now inside you when someone acknowledges a mistake and wants to make it up to you?

- Which relationships in your adult world have a similar flavor?

- What happens in your body when you see others treating each other with kindness, respect, tenderness, and care?

- What core beliefs do you carry that arise from being in these relationships or from observing others being cared for in this way?

Take lots of notes. Create a gallery of nondominant hand drawings that express the felt sense in your body of such nourishing encounters. Take as much time as you want with this practice and return to it often, especially in times when the work with attachment pain and fear is heavy. These inner anchors are the forever nourishment that we need in hard times.

The work we have been doing in this chapter is to help us connect the felt sense of our current relationships with their roots in the past. For much of our lives, we have mostly been on automatic pilot, so that when pain and fear threaten to flare up in a relationship, our wise protectors jump in to ward off this misery. Maybe I turn my back on you. Or maybe you yell at me. It is the nature of implicit memory that it feels like all the pain is coming from what is happening now, but together we are discovering that often the intensity of the feelings and even the feelings themselves are rooted in unhealed early attachment wounds. How do we break this cycle of relational destruction?

Slowing down to feel into the links between our protective adaptations and the wounds they are meant to guard us against builds our *inner caring observer*, that capacity to feel an implicit memory arising and witness it at the same time. One of the most significant changes in how we are in relationship with others is when, in the moment, we can sense that one of our protectors is with us because an implicit wound is being awakened in us. It is as though we can stand back a bit and witness our inner world rather than being swept away by it. In that moment, instead of immediately assigning responsibility for our feelings to the other person (romantic partner, child, parent, friend, co-worker), we find we can pause to be curious about where the feelings might be coming from. Turning to whomever is supporting us in this healing time, we can let our bodies guide us back to the early wounds that are stirring and bring the disconfirming experience our Little Me needs.

With consistent practice, you will get more and more skilled at making these connections between current experiences and past wounds, bringing you a new kind of confidence in your relationships. The bewilderment of falling into old patterns repeatedly will give way to optimism about getting to the roots of whatever struggles may come. If you have a partner who is also interested in doing this work, some remarkable resolutions are often on the horizon.

HEALING TOGETHER

I had seen Stacy and Paul for a few months before they got married because Stacy's mother had unexpectedly died and they wanted support in their grief. Now they were back because they were in a constant struggle about how to parent their curious, outgoing two-year-old daughter. "I love you, Stacy, but if you continue to let her act up without getting her behavior in line, I don't think I can stay with you," Paul said in our second session together. Stacy was in tears as she said, "How can you threaten me like that? You promised you would never leave me—or us." For Paul, the issue really did seem to be about their daughter, Cherie. For Stacy, it seemed much more about her husband. Even though they were at an impasse, it was clear they loved each other and had both wanted to come see me to sort this out.

Paul said, "I'm not going to leave, honey. I just don't know how to get you to understand how important discipline and good behavior are to me. If we spoil her and she thinks she can do whatever she wants, she'll have a miserable life."

Stacy asked an important question. "Where is this coming from? You've been this loving, devoted father who seemed to enjoy every new thing she did. Now all of a sudden you want to put a fence around her. And you want it enough to threaten me."

Paul was silent and looked confused, so I suggested that Stacy's question might point us in a helpful direction. "When any of us have big reactions that don't make sense to us if we stop and think about them, asking 'Where is this coming from?' is often really helpful," I said. "Early on, we all learn what it takes to stay in connection with our all-important parents. Sometimes we can just be ourselves, but there are almost always also times when we're required to feel, think, and behave in certain ways because of our parents' needs."

I was going to say more, but Paul was shifting in his chair and looking down and away. Something was clearly stirring in him. As I paused, he said, "Our family story is that I was a good kid until I refused to stay in the house. I was a little older than Cherie and got obsessed with going outside to make mud and build stuff. Even though we all laugh about it now, it's also true that my father began to hit me every time I made a move for the back door. I haven't thought about it in years. Right now it doesn't feel so funny."

I asked Paul if we could be with this boy inside. He nodded yes. As we got closer to his child, I saw Paul's hand move to his belly and asked what he was feeling in his body. "An ache, right here," he said, "and my head hurts and I feel really scared. I love my dad, but I love outdoors, too. And I don't understand why he's hitting me." His body cringed into the corner of his chair. Stacy had moved her chair closer to Paul and took his hand, which seemed to allow years of unshed tears to flow. We just stayed with this little boy, wanting only to witness the truth of his experience. Paul's belly gradually softened, and then the memory faded.

The next time they came in, he shared that he still felt terribly anxious when Cherie got what he called "overexcited," but now he knew where these intense sensations were coming from. He was a little frustrated that knowledge hadn't taken care of the feelings. I said, "The first big step in changing these patterns comes when our caring observer can see the origin. But just understanding doesn't change the implicit memory. We need to continue to follow your body to the memories that are holding these big feelings in place. We need to continue to be with that sad, scared little boy." And so we did. For about six months.

During this time, we were also attending to all that had been awakened in Stacy by Paul's threat to leave. Even though he had taken it back almost immediately, her inner world, so filled with abandonment as a child, couldn't unhear it. As she described the terror welling up from her belly all the way to her eyes, he came close to attend to her little one. They were each other's constant companions in this work, beautiful co-anchors that were at the center of this healing process.

I wanted to finish this chapter by sharing a little of Stacy and Paul's story because our intimate relationships can become such a foundation for the deepest healings. Two people (sometimes with the support of a third person, like a therapist or trusted friend) amplify the safety that can hold the pain and fear of early losses. The opposite is also true. If both people aren't ready to step into the work, we also need to do what is necessary to provide safety for all the parts of ourselves. We'll explore this in the next chapter.

3

LIVING IN HEARTFELT CONNECTION

CHAPTER 7

KNOWING WHEN TO STAY—
AND WHEN IT'S TIME TO GO

A s we move into the final section of this book, we will continue to draw on the meditations we developed to help process and heal our implicit memories in part 2. They are intended to be lifelong practices that we visit frequently. These practices lie at the heart of our journey toward emotional health and are the foundation for building warm, safe relationships. At my own point in this work, I know that I will keep listening to my body and to the voice of my Little Me for the rest of my life. It has become as natural as brushing my teeth to be curious about what is happening in my inner world, and to reach out for support from my inner and outer anchors when I need it. As we travel along the last leg of this journey together, it is my hope that this will become natural for you, too.

As we move through our lives, our implicit world is often calling more of the shots than we are consciously aware of. Like a pair of glasses with colored lenses, our implicit memories shape how we see our experiences with others and our expectations for how we believe relationships "should" be. These expectations can guide us—again and again—toward what is familiar. Our work together is changing the shading in these glasses. When we have had the gift of secure attachment or are working our way toward that security now, our embodied expectation is that there will be closeness and acceptance in our relationships. Even when there is a rupture in a connection—the inevitable disappointment or disagreement we all have with the people we love from time to time—we expect the rupture will quickly be repaired. As a result, our implicit world has a tendency to lead us toward relationships that feel similarly safe and secure. At the other end of the spectrum, if our early life has left us with the felt sense that relationships are full of chaos, fear, or abandonment, we are often drawn toward people who, sadly, can provide us only with this kind of unsafe, distressing experience.

Pause for Reflection

Take a moment to see if any difficult relationships, which might not feel safe, come to mind. They might be ones that you are currently in, or ones that have broken apart in the past. When you think of this person or people, what feelings come up in your body? Do you feel tightness or constriction in your chest, or perhaps there is a sensation of unease in

> your belly, or tension in particular groups of muscles? It can
> be helpful to make some notes in your journal about the
> feelings that come up in your body when you think of these
> experiences.

SEARCHING FOR "THE ONE"

After several relationships that brought her nothing but heartache, one of my clients said to me with a sad smile on her face, "My picker's broken!" Her attempt at a small joke about something that obviously pained her made my heart ache for her. She had such a deep sense that she was incapable of recognizing any person—friend or lover—capable of being in a mutually safe, healthy relationship. Indeed, our attachment wounds from the past can continue to pull us toward relationships in which painful and sometimes dangerous dynamics wreak havoc on our sense of safety, activating our nervous system and changing our neurochemicals. It is a sad truth that when our traumas are guiding our sense of attraction, we can mistake these "gut feelings" of intense connection for a genuine intuition that a person who is wrong for us is "the one." When my client reflected to me that she thought she just didn't have the ability to choose the right partners, we were at the beginning of our time together and her unhealed wounds, which were still unconscious, were the primary guide she had in choosing lovers. In our work together, she learned how to untangle her past from her present so that she could go forward trusting that there was nothing wrong with her "picker."

In this chapter, we are going to explore why sometimes romantic relationships that seem to start well end up touching on our deep wounds or those of a potential mate. As we have seen, sometimes our companion has no interest or ability to join us in getting the therapeutic help we both need. In this chapter, we will dig into what we need to feel safe in relationship and why leaving behind what feels unsafe can be so hard. The challenging truth is that even when we are able to recognize the painful cycle in which we're caught, it can be so terribly difficult to actually make the move to leave. We'll begin by tracing the stages of a relationship in order to understand more deeply how to know when it's truly time to go—or when there is the possibility of mutual healing with your partner.

HOW RELATIONSHIPS DEVELOP

Each relationship is unique, but at the same time, there are tendencies that apply to the development of most relationships. In general, the more profound our developmental trauma, the greater the odds that our attraction to someone in the beginning stems from old wounds. One of my clients, Louisa, shared this awareness with me after we had spent a number of months together. "When I go toward a new friendship, it's like the healthiest parts of me show up. When I feel drawn to a guy, I can feel how the parts of me who watched my parents trash each other come flying to the surface to do the choosing, and I wind up with people who only seem to thrive when there is conflict and have no idea how to be close."

As we talked more about her experiences in relationship, some of her implicit and explicit memories came alive. "My mom had a group of really close friends who were often at our house through my whole childhood. I feel a warmth spread all over my chest just picturing them in our living room and kitchen in my mind." We sat with that feeling for a while, enjoying the security and peacefulness she felt as she remembered being in their company. Suddenly I saw a sadness come over her. "I'm remembering the bad times came when I was alone with my parents. I wish I'd had a brother or sister. It seems like it would have been better if I'd had someone to share it all with." She paused and then went on. "I got so tense when I heard my father's car in the driveway. I'd look at my mother and could feel her gearing up for a fight. Almost before he got in the door, she was criticizing him. Never one to take it lying down, he used his big brain to try to level her. They never hit each other, but they also never seemed to love each other. And all the while, they didn't have any time for me. I don't think they even knew that their incessant arguing was having an effect on me. I spent so much time alone in my room." We sat with the sadness for a bit and then Louisa leaned back to take me on a long visit with her latest relationship. "When I met Andre, I was sure this one would be different. He showered me with attention and sweet small gifts. His compliments were extravagant. Could he really like *everything* about me? At the beginning, we were in a long-distance relationship, so we started off texting throughout the day. Even after we were physically together, there was a lot of contact by phone and text. There was never one word of criticism."

This was the blissful honeymoon phase where the neurochemicals dopamine, serotonin, and oxytocin weave a spell of infatuation, making everything our partner does seem charming. Brain research has given us insights into the blindness these neurochemicals can induce. There is nothing wrong with a surge of chemistry going off in our brains and bodies. In fact, it's adaptive as we begin to establish a bond with a new person in our lives. If we have a great deal of attachment trauma, however, this chemical flood is also protective to give us the best chance of making a strong connection before the inevitable arising of implicit memories can derail us. This is why Andre's care felt so good to Louisa's Little Me, who had been so wounded by her parents' cruelty to each other and their complete ignoring of her suffering.

Before too long, Louisa and Andre were sharing about their childhoods. Louisa learned that both of Andre's parents had been very demanding, requiring him to live up to their expectations in school and at home. Behavior and achievement were everything, and the cost of failure was severe. He was very clear that their love and attention came at the price of his not having any needs or desires outside the parameters his parents established. There was no safe way to be himself. He did say that his relationship with his brother was a saving grace for him. Most days they would run around in the woods near their home, and it was in these moments that he felt free. As Louisa shared this with me, I felt a great sorrow for Andre but also a sense of concern for how the lack of secure attachment in Andre's own life might impact Louisa at some point in their relationship.

In their initial excitement for each other, they felt they were standing on new ground where both of them were safe, cherished, and loved exactly as they were. From my perspective, I could see how their Little Mes were basking in the yearned-for unconditional love they had missed as children. This fantasy of unbroken bliss feels so real and necessary to people whose attachment pain has left them longing for a return to the innocence of childhood. Each wants the other to be the perfect parent of their imagination, to make up for what they needed but didn't get, and to protect them from being overwhelmed by the awakening of the pain and fear of their early losses.

No matter how great our need for nothing to change, some circumstance always comes along to break into this fantasy. Even if nothing dramatic happens, it is natural for the initial passion and fascination to make room for more of daily life. These changes often prompt the entry into the next phase of the relationship. Because some initial trust has been established, other aspects of ourselves begin to appear. "Will they still love me even if I get angry?" "Will they be able to stay with me if I feel insecure?" We don't necessarily ask these questions consciously, but underneath, we need to find out how much of ourselves can safely show up in the relationship. It's also true that our attachment wounds, bubbling underneath the surface, have always been sharply focused on any hint of changes in the relationship. As things inevitably shift, these traumatic implicit memories begin to awaken.

Louisa told me that about six or seven months into their relationship, the demands at Andre's job intensified when he got a promotion. Initially, this was a cause for celebration. "Our lives were right on track," she said, "so I was shocked when he began to come home angry. I didn't realize what was happening. Because of his preoccupation with work, I missed him in ways that made me terribly anxious, and I told him so, imagining that he would comfort me. Instead, he took it as I was telling him he was doing something wrong. After all the work you and I have done, now I understand that he was caught between the needs of my unsafe and insecure Little Me, his inner parents' command that he make exceptional progress at work, and his own inner child's anguish as he felt us coming apart. In an impossible bind, his anger showed up as a protector. But in that moment, all I felt was our devotion for each other going up in flames. The pain and fear were so intense that I begged him not to be angry with me, and that drove him into more of a rage. That was the last straw for me, and my own rage woke up."

This second stage of relationship may shake up our sense of safety, but has the potential to deepen our bonds with each other. If each person has had some security in their childhood, they often have the bandwidth to accommodate—and perhaps even find endearing—the "warts and all" of the other person, mostly because that kind of acceptance is what they experienced from their parents as children. It doesn't mean there is no conflict, but when there is, it is met with more curiosity than judgment, and repairs often come quickly and easily.

Couples like Louisa and Andre, whose attachment foundations were severely disrupted, had no implicit patterns of safety and security to fall back on when the challenges arrived. Instead, they were swamped with implicit memories of the pain and fear of their childhoods. When difficulties arise in the present moment and also awaken old memories from childhood, the sensations are intense. Since Louisa and Andre weren't aware that some of their response was coming from the past, it was the most natural thing in the world for them to blame each other for their misery. Andre: "All you do is pull on me and criticize me!" Louisa: "You're mad at me all the time and don't even think about me anymore!" What many might call a power struggle is actually just two people desperately trying to fend off the intolerable feelings of loss and abandonment that are threatening their inner stability.

After about a month of this unrelenting misery, Louisa's friend suggested the two of them needed help. Louisa agreed, but Andre, completely overwhelmed by the demands of work and the terrible feelings welling up inside, said he couldn't imagine adding a therapy appointment to his schedule. I can appreciate the time crunch he was experiencing, but also believe his refusal was more about him needing to stay away from the anguish inside. That's when the relationship ended. Louisa and I continued, now working through the loss of her relationship with Andre and all that the experience had awakened in her.

Often as we transition from the euphoria of the honeymoon stage to the next stage of the relationship, we find ourselves at a fork in the road. For Louisa and Andre, the only path was breaking apart. But the inevitable conflict in relationships doesn't have to spell the end for the partnership. These struggles can be opportunities for growth, helping us hone our skills with rupture and repair, which will always lead to deeper connection. If we are able to navigate the discomfort with awareness, commitment, trust, and respect, the intimacy with our partner can expand in the most marvelous way. For many of us, this involves significant inner work, often supported by therapy, as we disentangle our past from our present while at the same time increasing our compassion for our partner. We can see it as an opportunity to welcome more and more parts of ourselves into the relationship. As we mature together, we realize that relationships aren't intended to be a perpetual high, but the ground on which we become more conscious, more healed, and ultimately more connected through the struggles as well as the joys.

However, sometimes the attachment wounds are so deep that the relationship becomes primarily a repetition of agonizing old patterns of disruption and disconnection. Louisa felt like she was living back in her family, where she was abandoned and nonexistent in the midst of her parents' fights, and Andre was equally nonexistent in the no-man's-land of having to sacrifice himself for everyone else's needs again. As is usually the case, both of their inner protectors took over to insulate them from the intolerable pain and became the dominant participants in the relationship, drowning out the sweetness and safety of the initial connection. Yet, despite all the anger that arose between them in the end, they were good-hearted people. They separated by mutual agreement.

I have spoken with many individuals and couples who have experienced dynamics similar to Louisa and Andre, but I am here to tell you that, as painful as this passage can be, with some individual healing work, there is every reason to believe that most people can someday find a fulfilling relationship. But for some, there are very early attachment wounds that require the individual to develop the kind of inner protectors that can make healing unlikely and relationships extremely painful (although I hold hope for everyone).

LOST IN THE CHAOS OF OUR EARLIEST ATTACHMENTS

For some people, in addition to having their most basic attachment needs unmet, they have also suffered abuse. This can leave an ocean of pain and fear that causes them to attempt to avoid it at all costs. These individuals can adapt by developing a team of inner protectors and outer behaviors to ward off their sea of anguish in ways that, unfortunately, often harm others. Their inability to trust others means that anyone in a relationship with them will feel intensely diminished, unknown, used, and abused. Hell for everyone. In this section we will explore how the devastating wounds from attachment trauma and abuse can impact certain people and the difficulty this can present for the people who love them.

Psychologists and others use the term *borderline* to describe a group of behaviors that are hard to tolerate when we are in relationship with a person suffering in this way. Adolph Stern first coined the term to describe patients who didn't seem to fit into any neat box in terms of their grasp on reality. Was this neurotic behavior (where the person has some sense of how their perceptions are based in anxiety or neurosis) or psychotic behavior (where the person's grip on reality has largely disappeared)? From my experience,

I think it is more accurate to call this a "complex post-traumatic response to extreme attachment loss in infancy." Suffice to say that parents who have a lot of chaotic disorganized attachment are unable to provide their little ones with a calming presence, safe contact, or accurate reflection. Instead, their babies take in their parents' frightening disorganization while having nowhere they can land to feel secure. It's this dramatic lack of safety that sets the stage for split-second terror to wake up in them at the slightest sign of abandonment. If we can imagine a baby screaming and flailing in their crib, all alone, this is akin to what is going on underneath this adult's dramatic behavior. It's important to recognize that none of these responses are their fault or under their control.

To be in a relationship with someone who suffers in this way is to be idealized one moment and seen as the devil the next. Their need for soothing is insatiable and unsatisfiable because of the magnitude of the chaos inside. Meanwhile, none of it makes sense to their partner because the reactions feel so out of proportion to the actual circumstances. And yet, for the wounded person, all their dramatic outbursts are springing from the vast implicit chasm of terror. We are all at the mercy of our perceptual universe, and for someone with these kinds of wounds, the world feels continually dangerous in life-threatening ways. The response to such inner torture can include thoughts about or even attempts of suicide and acts of self-harm, extending the terror to all those around them.

People who were caretakers for emotionally unstable or frightening parents when they were children are often drawn to people with this magnitude of wounding. The feeling of having the impossible task of calming the uncalmable person is so familiar, even if repeating the past is its own kind of hell. And yet these bonds sometimes endure until the caregiving person collapses. Or things can escalate to the point that the two people are caught up in a cycle of physical or emotional abuse. The odds of these two people being able to settle into a fulfilling relationship without lots of individual help are minimal.

Fortunately, in the late 1970s, Marsha Linehan, a woman who had suffered from the kinds of wounds that cause borderline traits to emerge, developed a form of therapy called Dialectical Behavior Therapy, or DBT, often practiced in groups, which can help people with these struggles begin to heal. Other therapists offer treatment in individual therapy for these deep wounds, drawing on relational neuroscience's insights about severe developmental trauma. It is important to say again that as hard as it is to be around the behaviors that result from such traumatic circumstances, none of this is the person's fault. They in fact need and deserve the most thoroughgoing empathy and compassion for their suffering.

Providing the kind of intense care that people with borderline personality disorder require can be a rough road for partners who are seeking a more mutually supportive relationship. However, a therapist with both deep understanding and a well-developed neuroception of safety can hold a space in which healing can unfold. In truth, both the person who experienced such abandonment and the one who has taken on the role of caretaker need extensive care and support, particularly nonjudgmental holding and reflection to help their brains rewire in ways that will change how they feel, see, and relate in the world.

◎

KAYA'S TENDER HEART

When Kaya came to see me, she said she needed someone to help her with the person she had been partnered with for the last two years. I could feel her confusion and desperation. "I love Peter so much, but he is becoming more and more distraught, and I am not sure what I can do to help him. I am so exhausted. Some days I can't focus on work. My stomach and head hurt in ways they never have before. But he's not okay—and now I'm not, either. When I mention the possibility of even a few hours apart, Peter says he will kill himself if I go. And I believe him! He tried several times before I met him. In a sense, I believe it is even part of what drew me to him. He is such a beautiful, tender person, and he deserves to be with someone who sees him that way. He pleads with me to stay, tells me I'm his angel, and then he's enraged at me for reasons I don't understand, and then turns it on himself. I've tried everything I can think of."

In those first couple of sessions, we simply spent time with the trapped feeling she was having while she told me stories about her relationship with Peter. Her misery wasn't only about being afraid to take a little space, but also about her genuine anguish at abandoning this man she loved and deeply understood. She told me about his history of living with and caring for a mother living with schizophrenia, whose threats of violence and suicide kept him in a terrified state all the time. Before Peter was born, his father had taken refuge in alcohol to avoid his mother, leaving Peter in charge from the time he was small. No wonder Kaya's heart was breaking for him.

As we continued meeting, I began to ask her to share something of her own childhood experience. The thing that told me the most about what was happening for her was her inability to stay with my question for even a moment. Her attention and energy were immediately drawn back to Peter. When I gently mentioned this to her, her head dropped and she looked away. In a small voice, she said, "I didn't mean to do anything wrong."

"Oh, no! You didn't do anything wrong at all," I said. "It just seems that there isn't any room for you to share yourself with me."

She seemed bewildered, as though my words made no sense. "But it's Peter who's in danger . . ."

After a moment's silence, I softly asked, "I wonder if there have been other times in your life when you've been close to someone else who has been in danger?"

It got densely quiet for a moment. Then, "Every day." We took a few breaths together. And she began—with her mother.

She had fled from a war-torn country in Africa before Kaya was born. The journey to the US was dangerous and she arrived pregnant, the victim of a rape that occurred at the hands of those who were helping them flee. Kaya told me that what she remembered most from being a child was the look of terror on her mother's face whenever something unexpected happened. She and her mom were part of a small community of refugees, and her mother soon became attached to one of the men in the community. It wasn't about love, but survival. As she told me about this, I could see her entire body tensing. After a pause, she said, "They were all like wounded children, you know. The men and the women. Not an adult among them. So those of us who really were children took over."

As she shared her history with me, I understood more deeply the power of the bond she was experiencing with Peter. The attachment wounds they suffered caring for their frightened and disabled mothers were so similar that some would refer to their connection as a trauma bond. People bonded by trauma in this way identify with their partner's pain to the point that they become lost in it. Having this type of deep empathy for each other's early attachment wounds can lead to blurred boundaries and self-abandonment as they attempt to heal each other's Little Me without being able to attend to their own pain and suffering. Among spiritual communities, the term *twin flame* is used to describe these intensely overlapping injuries, the thought being that twin flames are a single soul split into two as a catalyst for healing each other. The hallmark is the intensity of the relationship. Whether we want to see Kaya and Peter through these lenses or simply as two people whose profoundly similar wounds were magnetic for each other, it is clear that the strong radar of familiarity was powerfully at work.

During childhood, Kaya formed a close bond with two other young girls in the community, and she believes that saved all of them from losing their minds with the effort to somehow help their mothers. The three of them split their lives into two parts, one part intent on keeping their dissociated and suicidal mothers from dying and the other part focused on becoming part of American society. Probably because they had each other's support, they succeeded at both.

Now I saw before me an accomplished and strong young

woman of twenty-seven who longed to be in a loving relationship. She and Peter clearly cared deeply about each other, and yet the magnitude of his needs were threatening her own inner balance and her health. It was clear to me that this relationship was awakening the pain and terror of her attachment to her mother in overwhelming ways, as her daily life was filled with this all-too-familiar sense of complete responsibility for another.

The magnitude of this bind was a hard one for me to sit with. My left hemisphere wanted to say to Kaya, "You aren't responsible for whether he lives or dies. You didn't cause the wounds that have left these feelings in him. You must take care of yourself." But that would have diminished or ignored the genuineness of the bond between them, leaving her alone with the anguish within her. Instead, we began to be with her Little Me inside, who had kept Mom alive, trusting that as she healed, she would find her right answer about staying with Peter or leaving.

One of the most important pieces of this healing work for Kaya was to have support. She and the two friends who had endured this traumatic childhood together were still close. Prior to this, none of them had been in therapy, but the strength of their bond and commonality of their experience made them strong anchors for each other. For the first time, they began to have conversations about what those years had actually been like. I don't know if they would have used this word, but I believe they were finding safety with each other, and it was opening long-locked doors.

Work of this kind had to move slowly, respectfully, carefully so that the pain and terror being released didn't overwhelm Kaya's daily life. It didn't take her long to realize that she was reliving her childhood in the relationship with Peter. But that knowledge alone didn't change the strength of her attachment to him or her feelings of complete responsibility for his survival. That was the work of months and years. Following a process very similar to the practices in chapters 4, 5, and 6, we began to come into visceral contact with the sea of early implicit memories that had been keeping her locked into the familiar pattern with Peter.

Over our two years together, Kaya separated from and returned to Peter several times. The pull of our deepest implicit convictions rarely releases all at once. When she was with him, the neuroception of danger—felt mostly in her belly—made her want to leave. When they were apart and she was no longer viscerally afraid, her belly became quiet, and the neuroception of safety she was feeling connected her to the love in her heart. The neuroception we are having in any particular moment is a powerful force, and as Kaya's system went from danger to safety, she followed its prompting and returned. Their relationship had never been physically abusive, but this push and pull between the neuroception of danger and safety is the same process that makes it so difficult for people in domestic violence relationships to go and stay gone. We may often judge them—or ourselves—for going back, but there are powerful forces at work internally that are stronger than logic.

Through this messy, unpredictable healing process, the intense danger Kaya's inner world experienced every day with her mother was gradually transforming into a neuroception of increasing inner safety as her Little Me came to live more in the present moment with her trusted friends and with me. One moment of implicit healing at a time, her perception changed enough so that she could more consistently see and feel that being knotted up in the terror of saving Peter wasn't good for either of them.

Kaya was, of course, eager for Peter to experience the healing that was happening for her, but his inner world kept that door closed. I don't know if it was because he didn't have the kind of friendships in childhood that had been a saving grace for Kaya, or simply the inner sense that he wouldn't survive exposure to the feelings of his younger years. As hard as it is, we need to respect the wisdom that lives in each person.

Even though she continued to care for Peter, Kaya realized she needed to make a clean break because the sense of "maybe" was torture for both of them. As kindly as she could, she let him know that she couldn't keep in touch. Of course, it isn't easy to know that we will never again see someone we have loved this deeply for this long. The thought of it is hard, and the actuality of it often wakes up implicit memories of abandonment in a very deep way. The depth of her embodied grief surprised Kaya. "How can it be that I know for sure this is the right course and it still feels like torture?"

Out of years of experience, both personal and with my clients, I said, "We have done so much work with the pain and fear of having to save your mother every day, but I don't know that we've fully touched the other part of your Little Me who needed her mother to see her and love her. Even though it is your choice, leaving Peter still means a terrible loss of love. I believe that has awakened your Little Me's need for such tender closeness. She's here with us now, and we will stay with her as long as she needs."

WOUNDED AND WOUNDING

The earliest attachment wounds sometimes create the kind of relational patterns that Kaya and Peter experienced. When shame is more than disorganization at the root of the wound, a different kind of pattern often emerges, one that leaves the person with narcissistic tendencies. Shame is considered by many to be one of the two most painful emotions. (The other is extreme anxiety.)

> ### *Pause for Reflection*
>
> Let's take a moment to see if a time when you felt ashamed or humiliated comes into your mind. What do your eyes, your head, your chest, your belly, and your muscles want to do? What is the word that comes immediately to mind? If you find yourself focusing on a moment from your childhood, what did the Little Me inside of you feel? Small? Tender? Alone? What feelings come to mind?

From the time we are born, we depend on the reflection of our parents to gain a sense of who we are and what the world expects of us. Avoidant parents struggle to see us beyond the litany of physical requirements they have to meet as parents—to feed us and make sure there is a roof over our heads. Ambivalent parents are present with us sometimes and at other times are swept up in their own world. This swinging back and forth happens unpredictably and creates anxiety in their baby. Disorganized parents who vacillate between extremes—in one moment desperate for affirmation that they are loved and in other moments distancing themselves from any kind of connection—leave a legacy of confusion and terror inside their little ones. Sadly, some mixture of all three often lies within someone who is likely to become a narcissist.

For avoidant parents, we are a project to be completed or a burden to be carried rather than a child to be cherished. For ambivalent parents, we are someone who they unintentionally use to meet their own emotional needs. For disorganized parents, we are a receptacle for their terror. All of this sets the stage for the development of profound shame. We quickly feel that we aren't getting the kind of warmth and loving attention we need from our parent or parents because we are in some way flawed or not good enough. We come to believe that, due to some deficiency in ourselves, we don't deserve warmth or love. By the time we are toddlers, our brains have developed enough complexity to experience shame. So, like any healthy two-year-old, we dance around the room, squealing in delight, and looking to see if anyone or everyone is noticing us. The avoidant parent frowns at our behavior (I'm bad). The ambivalent parent signals for us to stop and attend to them (my needs don't matter). And the disorganized parent likely doesn't notice at all or joins us in an inappropriate way (terrifying disconnection). Unseen and uncared for, we feel an anguish of shame build up inside.

Now, as an adult, this person is still dancing around to try to compel people to look at them with delight. Desperate for attention so they don't feel the gaping hole of darkness and shame that was established when they were small, this person will do anything to be noticed. At the same time, their traumatized implicit world is convinced that the only possibility is further abandonment and invisibility. This intolerable bind can lead to all kinds of extreme behaviors. At the beginning of a relationship, it can look like love bombing—a river of extravagant gifts and gestures—and total attention that feels like full attunement. Underneath is a terrifying dread that can be so all-consuming it usually cuts off any ability on the narcissist's part to feel empathy for their partner. Even if they are able to sense what is happening inside the other person, they use this awareness to manipulate their partner so they won't be left.

As the initial neurochemicals induced by this flood of attention wear off, panic sets in for the one needing all eyes on them, often leading to attempts to control their partner. Many times, they will seek to isolate them from friends and family out of fear they will leave. Often, the adoration turns into criticism aimed outward before their partner can shame them. And sometimes the whole thing flips 180 degrees, with threatened abandonment leading the partner to beg the narcissist to stay. Or the narcissist may flip back and forth between full attention and abandonment, creating a kind of intermittent reinforcement that actually makes it harder to leave than either full focus or full rejection. The abandoned partner can be left waiting, trained to beg for and expect the return, frozen within a relationship that provides no emotional safety whatsoever.

Looking at this from the outside, as I view my clients' lives, I can sense the utter desperation fueling these destructive protections. Viewed from inside my own experience, I remember the feeling of both suffocation and excited fulfillment in the initial stages, switching to the terror of complete abandonment as my partner withdrew from me. I was vulnerable to this person because my own attachment wounds left me craving exactly the kind of attention he initially offered. I was hooked, very much like a fish struggling in the control of the one who had caught me.

Just like all of us but to a more extreme degree, narcissists have fine-tuned radar for what is familiar in relationship, coupled with protectors who will do anything to ward off experiencing the disastrous bodily sensations and emotions inside. All of this has a chemical and brain development component, too. The neurochemicals of trust, love, calmness, and empathy have been thrown out of balance in infancy, through no fault of the child, and the brain connections necessary for empathy and self-reflection, which develop only through tender treatment from parents, are tragically diminished or absent. This also means that it is unlikely that someone suffering in this way will seek treatment. All their efforts to survive are focused outward, so slowing down to turn inward feels impossible.

If you find yourself in this kind of relationship, the most important thing is to remain connected to friends and family so you aren't at the mercy of your own inner wounds and the narcissist's infinite needs. Reaching out toward those who can accompany you in your own healing will help to protect you from being drawn into this kind of relationship again.

◎

JAMES'S IMPOSSIBLE DILEMMA

Not all narcissistic wounds create the same behaviors, though the roots are similar and the outcome for the other person often follows the pattern described above. We are all pretty familiar with the kind of full-blown outrageous acting-out-for-attention that characterizes some people in the public eye. When James came to me, he was dealing with something different. He thought he was there for a practical reason. "I need strategies to deal with my mother," he said. He went on to describe how she had simply shown up at his condo and said she would be living there from now on. "She acted as though I should be delighted. There was no question in her mind that this is what was going to happen. Embarrassed as I am to say this, I pretty much had a panic attack and stepped out of the way to let her in." He paused for a moment, looking at me intently. Then he went on, "I live in a one-bedroom condo. It's spacious but still only one bathroom, one bedroom, a very large living space, nice kitchen. But one bedroom. Do you get it?" Yes, I was getting it. I nodded, and just as I was preparing to speak, he went on, "She's been there for two weeks. I'm sleeping in the living room, getting up very early to be sure I can get into the bathroom in time to get to work, and she's acting like everything's just fine. How do I get her out?"

I said something like, "That's a big question, and I understand your urgency. I believe if there was an obvious answer to that, you would have already discovered it. So maybe we need to back up a little bit before we try and answer this question. What do you think?" It's possible that the sound of my welcoming voice was helping him slow down a little. With a deep sigh, he said, "Okay."

"I'm kind of back with the part where you said you had a panic attack when she showed up," I said.

"You would, too, if you'd been living around her for fifty years like I have. Fifty years of her cheerfully ruling every roost, always getting what she wants, never caring—not even for a second—about what it means for someone else. My siblings were smart. They moved out of the country, all of them." He was trying for humor, one of the best protectors in impossible situations. With a sly smile, he said, "A brick wall is cushy compared to her obliviousness." I believe he could feel that I was listening closely.

Slowing down, he continued, "This latest episode came about because the man she'd been living with had had enough and threw her out. She's never had money of her own, so she had no place to go—except to me." It was easy for me to feel the magnitude of the bind he was in.

Looking at me directly, he asked, "What am I supposed to do? She's my mother."

"Yes, and just imagining saying no to her brings you to panic." I thought, *What an awful dilemma.* I knew we would be up against his need for an immediate solution while what his system really needed was a long, slow healing of the profound attachment trauma he experienced with a mother who was completely unable to acknowledge his existence. I wondered who may have annihilated her like that. He was so used to it that it just seemed normal at one level, and yet his deeply human self, for whom connection is a biological imperative, was agonized by the cheerful neglect. Pain, anger, and panic were the result.

That was the end of our first meeting together. By the time he returned, I knew I needed to let him know that the answer to his question was most likely going to emerge when the younger parts of him no longer felt the panic of this impossible bind. Each time his mother arrived on his doorstep, his neglected Little Me woke up and his adult self receded. When there is a lot of unhealed trauma, this is what happens to most of us. Then the conversation, feelings, and actions were actually happening between his mother and this young child. I trusted that if we could be with James's Little Me, giving him safe haven for healing, he would be able to remain an adult and the situation would have some chance of resolving itself differently.

One thing we had on our side was his well-developed left hemisphere. I felt sure he would be able to focus on what I was saying and understand it intellectually. As we talked about what would be needed for him to heal, it felt like an alliance was building. This alone would be healing because this kind of joining is exactly what was impossible with his mother. I asked him how it would be to have her there for a while longer while we focused on his healing. Instead of asking "How much longer?" he simply said, "Yes."

I didn't hear much about his mother over the next few months. He was sometimes staying with a friend or taking a weekend away, creatively relieving the constant pressure of being in his overoccupied home. When he was away, it also gave him the privacy he needed to grieve the agonizing wounds of having been so thoroughly ignored by his mother for his whole life. When he was with trustworthy friends, he had the accompaniment he needed to be able to talk about what it was like to be a child whose very existence wasn't acknowledged. He found he wasn't the only one who had experienced that with parents so preoccupied with their own world and their own wounds that their children were an afterthought at best.

And we were sitting together, week after painful week. As trust and safety built between us, James's system made room for him to fall, over and over again, into the tormenting sensations that such emotional neglect creates. It's hard to describe what happens to a person's inner world because this kind of neglect can seem like it should be felt as a nothingness. And indeed, initially James experienced himself sitting in a vast dark room, completely alone. As we were there with that child, bit by bit this protective darkness gave way to sensations of a rending, tearing dismemberment, a black hole into which he would fall eternally, and a sense of disappearance so intense that it felt like dying. The outwardly quiet trauma of emotional neglect can be even more devastating than obvious physical abuse. Even as I write this, I'm aware that a simple paragraph can't begin to capture the intensity of the work we needed to do during this transformative time.

After a few months, James began noticing that his body was starting to feel a little different around his mother. Before, he had felt himself shrinking away from her internally, literally getting small inside. When her lack of awareness of him was particularly strong, the panic would rise in his chest, and his belly would feel sick. Now James was recognizing that these sensations were his child's voice, telling him the truth about the pain of this relationship and simply asking to be heard. After months of us listening to and holding his Little Me close, he had internalized me so we were more of an inner team on behalf of his young one, too. While the process was uneven—sometimes he could stay in his adult self, sometimes not—overall he felt steadier around his mother.

He said he didn't feel closer to making a decision about what to do in a practical sense, but for the first time in his life he didn't feel agitated around her even though she was her usual heedless self. "She's just a little girl, isn't she?" he said. The stories he had heard of her childhood felt like distant fairy tales with no substance, so he didn't know what she really experienced when she was younger. She was estranged from everyone in her family, leaving him completely in the dark about what had happened to all of them. "I don't suppose the facts matter. The whole story is really about the way she wasn't able to be my mother." A kind of mature and beautiful sadness was growing in him now in the place of the panic and desperation.

James decided that he had done the work he needed to do with me, so we gently parted. He was beginning to have some creative ideas about how to resolve the living situation with his mother, but didn't feel he needed my support to make it happen. It's amazing how healing deep and long-held trauma liberates the mind's creativity.

During our time together, James had also told me about several partners he'd had for fairly brief periods of time. All of the men he was drawn to had two things in common: after an intense period of passionate connection, they turned out to be incredibly self-centered and they were continually critical of him. He said, "It was that last part, the cruel criticism, that told me to get out fast." These partners were much more the typical expression of narcissism—criticism, control, and self-importance—than his mother had been. Ironically, the fact that she wasn't critical probably saved him from getting stuck in these painful relationships. These men just didn't feel familiar enough to his implicit world for him to get sucked into their world. We both had to smile about that.

As we begin to get a sense of what it is like to be with someone with borderline or narcissistic traits, it is so important to remember that each person is an individual with a unique attachment history and adaptations that take into account their temperament and the degree of their wounding. Some will be able to get help and others won't. This has little to do with conscious choice. It is more a matter of whether each person's inner world believes they can survive touching the fire inside. But until they are able to find the support that helps them feel safe enough to slowly, slowly approach the anguish, healthy relationship will likely remain out of reach for them. Their inner world is so dramatically and continually unsafe that they can't offer safety and security to anyone else.

With all our emphasis on the attachment wounds of infancy and beyond, it can be easy to blame parents for what happens to us. I used to lean that way, but it has become increasingly clear to me (thanks to relational neuroscience and personal healing) that each of us lives in an intergenerational stream of experiences, some of them warm, connecting, and filled with hope; some of them soaked in distress, anguish, and fear. It doesn't do us any good to vilify our parents or call them toxic because it is we who ultimately will carry the anger and the feeling of being poisoned. Along the healing path, we will likely experience just about every possible emotion. I have been angry, grief-stricken, heartsick, jealous, and so much more. I have learned to not stop there, but to reach back through the generations, always with the support of trustworthy anchors, to *find and bring healing to the ancestral roots of all this transmitted pain.* We'll be exploring a lot more about this life-giving work in the next two chapters. In closing, it is worth repeating here a very important aspect of this work: *we can't do it alone.* I suspect that one significant difference between Peter's inner world and the inner worlds of Louisa and Andre is that Peter had very few if any other relational experiences beyond his relationship with Kaya to offset his intolerable wounds. It made so much difference that Louisa had experienced her mother's joy in friendship and that Andre's body remembered the romps in the woods with his brother. These embodied memories and internalized relationships let them know that something other than the pain of the wounds with their parents was possible. It is easier to leave the door to healing open when we have had some safety and some hope and can look for more of the same in our adult relationships.

> Each of us lives in an intergenerational stream of experiences.

CHAPTER 8

WHAT HAPPENS WHEN WE HEAL?

A s we are nearing the end of our journey together, I'd like to check in with you on how you might be feeling at this point along your healing path. Do you feel your past slowly loosening its grip on your present? Are you leaning in more to the warm relationships that provide you with a felt sense of safety?

As I learned from my own experience with attachment losses, we can live our whole lives with our wounds running the show and dictating our life choices. Being at the mercy of our implicit injuries means unknowingly perpetuating cycles of pain and fear that can have lasting detrimental effects. By bringing our young wounds to light and holding them with care and support, we can free ourselves to make conscious decisions that lead to healthier, more fulfilling relationships and a richer, more connected life. I want to congratulate you on taking these important steps toward healing.

One of our most natural human tendencies is to try to solve our difficulties by changing something external. Hoping that we might somehow stumble upon a new outcome, we try and shift something in our outer world. We get a new partner, a new work environment, or "do a geographical" and move all the way across the country. And yet, in all these new situations, we take ourselves—our strengths and our wounds—with us. One of my clients said, "I literally moved to Costa Rica and found myself waiting for me there!" Well said. Unfortunately, the relief that comes from these outer changes is only temporary. Inevitably, the familiar patterns rise up again and often in the most emotionally vulnerable parts of our lives. It can be discouraging if not devastating to repeat the same cycle over and over again.

The truth is: *What we can't consciously feel, we tend to act out. And what we don't feel safe to act out, we try to suppress.* In the end, though, our wounds must go somewhere. Because our traumas live in our bodies, they impact our emotional *and* physical health. As trauma expert Bessel van der Kolk says, the body really does keep the score.

One of the primary ways suppressed traumas show up in the body is through inflammation. These fires in our body are the headwaters for all kinds of autoimmune, digestive, cardiac, and other chronic illnesses. Research suggests inflammation makes some cancers more likely as well. If we don't have enough support to be with our embedded traumas, our body makes what seems like a wise decision to simply hold the anguish in our physical system. Some of us have gone to great lengths to hide from our inner anguish until eventually the turmoil becomes so intense that the pain and fear find a way to break through. While these eruptions can be excruciating and frightening, they always arrive in search of healing.

Even when the emotional pain is enormous, with the right kind of support, it is possible to recover. When we can connect with others who can help us hold our suffering, we can begin to dedicate ourselves to the process of mending old wounds. The amazing thing is that the work you have been doing to heal your implicit memories through the practices in part 2 has been making changes in the actual circuitry in your brain. Relational neuroscience can help us understand what is actually happening "under the hood" that accounts for the changes you may be experiencing in the ways you feel, think, behave, and relate. As we explore the nature of these neural changes, we'll be pausing to reflect on what you may be noticing as your recovery process begins to blossom. Sharing these experiences with your anchors (trusted friends as well as the anchors within yourself) will help these new tendencies grow even deeper roots.

No matter the nature of our trauma, one of the deepest wounds we experience is feeling deeply alone when we are being hurt or ignored. Even if people are around, our pain and fear has gone unseen and untended. Now, when the care of another reaches all the way down into the neural nets holding those wounds, we internalize the person who is with us so we aren't alone anymore. This happens over time, easing the sense of abandonment. It is such a relief to be accompanied at last. At the same time, we are developing the implicit expectation that we will be lovingly accompanied. This is the foundation of feeling safe, and as this internalized sense of safety grows stronger and stronger, we will find ourselves drawn to partnerships who offer us this kind of connection rather than those who can never provide us with the felt sense of safety we crave. This change may be particularly noticeable when you connect with your Little Me. Having internalized many caring others, now you are able to find the same healing connection you have been experiencing with others inside yourself.

Pause for Reflection

If you can, return to a memory you have done some work with in previous chapters of this book to see if your Little Me now feels accompanied. Even if only some small bit of distress from the memory is lessened, feel into how much your little one now feels closer to one or more of your anchors as well as your adult self. The sensations in your body, especially around your heart, can often give you access to your sense of the presence or absence of connection. As best you can, simply notice, without judgment, how this is coming along. It can take some time for this sense of being held to become more solid and dependable. If you find your Little Me is still feeling alone, take a moment to reassure this young one of your intention to stay close and bring them other companions as well.

THE INTRICATE WEBS THAT CONNECT US

There is another aspect of being accompanied by a trustworthy anchor that expands our ability to feel safe enough to be truly open and available with others. We are powerfully affected by being with someone whose inner world is experiencing a neuroception of safety. As we discussed in chapter 1 (and will explore further in the Wisdom Notes at the end of the book), their autonomic nervous system is in a ventral state of safety that allows us to feel that we are welcome, that they are receptive to us. Whatever our own neuroception in that moment, as we sit together, our ANS becomes beautifully entangled with theirs, drawing us in the direction of also being in a state of safety. This is the essence of co-regulation. While our embedded traumas may have caused our ANS to be in sympathetic arousal or close to collapsing in shame or terror much of the time, as we join with our anchor, our inner state of safety can gradually grow stronger until it becomes baseline for us. This means that after something upsets us, we can more easily settle back into a felt sense of safety where we are naturally open to warm relationships with others. *A baseline of openness to connection* is one of the most important foundations for our sense of being safe in the world. Again, this is something that develops slowly, especially if we have had a lot of years of fear and hurt in our lives.

Pause for Reflection

Sensing the quality of your ANS takes practice, but perhaps you can begin by noticing what it is like to be with one of your anchors when you have something distressing to share. As this person receives you, listening with openness and care, what happens in your body? You might notice a shift in your breathing, your belly, your chest, or the quality of your muscles. These changing bodily sensations are the voice of your inner world communicating that they feel heard. If you find yourself slowing down, feeling more settled, you are likely moving into a neuroception of safety internally because you are playing the scales of warm engagement together.

The Subtle Art of Pausing

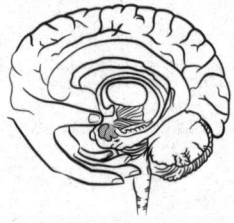

Not anatomically correct. When the connections between the orbitofrontal cortex (OFC), along with other prefrontal circuits, and the amygdala are strong, it is as though the OFC is a gentle hand providing soothing connection that slows our emotional reactivity.

Deep in our brains lie neural connections that have a major impact on how we relate with those who are closest to us. The little almond-shaped amygdala (shaded in the illustration) is the part of our brain that serves as a major processing center for our emotions. It also plays a major role in collecting our embodied experience and transforming it into the implicit memories that shape our perceptions and expectations about who we are and how our relationships will be. Near our amygdala is a part of our brain called the *orbitofrontal cortex* (OFC), symbolized by the hand below. These two are meant to work as a team to regulate our emotions, but they aren't connected to each other when we are born. The link between these two parts of the brain becomes strong when we are met by our parents with nonjudgmental warmth and loving curiosity, the relational qualities that create secure attachment.

If this kind of nurturing environment isn't available when we are young, the amygdala is left more on its own, with fewer connections to the OFC. Sensations of pain and fear from not being met as we need to be accumulate in the amygdala, ultimately becoming painful implicit memories we carry with us throughout our lives. Later in life, if we are fortunate enough to have safe people with us who can be truly present for us, we can touch the neural nets that hold these anguishing implicit memories, bringing healing to these early wounds. That allows this all-important circuitry to be established. The OFC and amygdala begin to hold hands. It is so lovely that *what didn't happen in childhood can be mended at any age.* These new links make pathways for the flow of the soothing neurochemical GABA between the OFC and amygdala, giving us a greater sense of calm. This makes a profound difference in so many ways.

The more our amygdala and orbitofrontal cortex work in partnership, the more we can pause when something happens that

> What didn't happen in childhood can be mended at any age.

wakes up a traumatic implicit memory in us. Instead of immediately responding with feelings and behaviors coming from the wound and from the way we have learned to protect ourselves from this kind of pain, we develop *inner space to reflect*.

Here's an example. Before these connections began to get solid in my brain, if my partner seemed less attentive, my inner world would well up with panic and I would begin to do all the frantic behaviors to keep him close. Now, as my amygdala and OFC are more linked, it is as though I can stand back a bit, recognize what's happening, and invite in comfort for this frightened child. This creates time to make a conscious decision about what I am going to do next. Neuroscientists tell us that before these neural connections are made, our responses unfold *100 times* faster than after they are made. That's an enormous difference. They call this new capacity *response flexibility*, which is a perfect phrase to capture this experience. It is such a relief to be so much less controlled by these wild feelings inside that had been with me since I was a young child.

Pause for Reflection

I have found the ability to pause before responding or acting to be one of the most encouraging signs that healing is

---

unfolding in my brain. This magic pause changes the quality of my relationships entirely. In order to get a sense of what pausing feels like, allow your mind and body to wander over some recent interactions you have had with a partner or close friend. If possible, have some of them come from before you began this work and some more recent interactions you have had while doing this work. Do you sense a pause developing when something challenging happens between the two of you? How is the felt sense of the interaction different? As with all things in healing, some days this is easier than others, so it is to be expected that there are still moments when the pause isn't available.

These new neural connections between the amygdala and OFC allow us to slow down and offer us neurochemical soothing. With greater emotional regulation, we are also able to experience a broad range of feelings and still remain steady. We don't need to shut down or lash out as much when strong emotions come up in us.

These linked circuits also affect the way we're able to be with others. We can listen more deeply, with increased empathy and compassion. There is room for more curiosity than judgment. We can also find more time to consider how we might help improve the lives of people in our broader community and the world.

Pause for Reflection

How comfortable are you with your strong emotions these days? Is it sometimes easier to be present with all of them? Again, this comes and goes for all of us, so we're just checking in with the overall trend. Are you becoming more at home with listening to others? And how about judgments? We all have them. But when they come up, are you a little more able to shift in the direction of curiosity about what is happening inside the other person? What is the felt sense in your body when you do that?

With the neural changes coming from our deeper connections with our anchors and with the resolution of our deep implicit wounds, what is really happening is that we are making our way back to our inherent health. As humans, we have evolved to be in warm, caring relationships with one another. It is only our embedded traumas that can stand in the way.

Rupture and Repair

All this doesn't mean that, with healing, all our close relationships will go smoothly every day. Far from it! What we can count on, however, is that our ability to make a repair and reconnect after things go awry will increase dramatically as we heal. This capacity is the secret sauce that makes any relationship more safe and secure. Every time there is a rupture (conflict) followed by a repair, we are building the implicit conviction that when things go wrong, they can be set right again.

In relationships, it takes two to repair. No matter how much I may want to make amends, it will happen only when the other person is willing, too. When it does, the feeling is almost always that something important has happened. My friend let me know that she was feeling disappointed in me because I'd been very distracted when we'd had dinner together. Two things happened inside me. I felt ashamed I had let her down and grateful she had said something. If shame had taken over, I would probably have defended myself and the opportunity for repair would have been lost. But we have a lot of trust between us, and I'm getting better at realizing I'm just a human being who screws up sometimes. I took a little deeper breath, reached for her hand, and said, "I'm so sorry. Yes, I was distracted and that mustn't have felt good to you. You matter to me, and the last thing I would want to do is not listen." I could feel her take a deeper breath, too, as we hugged each other. Because of these moments, trust continues to flourish between us, and that is the foundation for enduring friendship.

Perhaps you are remembering a time when someone offered an honest, heartfelt repair like that. Just take a moment to sense how your body experiences this. In mine, a good repair feels like hope, reassurance, confidence, and joy. I can screw up (I'm human), own it (I'm truthful), and seek to mend it (I'm open and vulnerable to you). What a great recipe for an increasingly intimate and safe relationship.

It feels wonderful when everything is rolling along smoothly, but actually, as neuroscientist Ed Tronick tells us, we make these thoroughly satisfying connections only about 33 percent of the time on the first try. All the rest is rupture and repair. This said, gaining skill at offering to mend things is pretty important. What does it take to get good at repair?

Moving Beyond Shame

As you grow more and more adept at accepting that mistakes and disconnections are an essential and even a valuable part of life, it's important to learn how to be with and heal the pools of shame that reside in most of us. It is shame that usually causes us to quickly get defensive, blame others, and get into a fight about who's right and wrong. All that does is deepen the initial rupture.

During the process of healing these pockets of shame, we will most likely develop compassion for ourselves and for the ones who humiliated us because of their own wounds, be they parents, friends, teachers, or workmates. When we do this accompanied by someone who offers us the sanctuary of acceptance just as we are, our inner shame morphs into a kind of quiet embrace for the little ones who suffered in this way. As a result, when someone comes at us in an accusing way or when we make a mistake or unkind remark, we may feel an initial urge to withdraw or attack, but it is quickly replaced by the felt sense of the suffering behind the meanness in us or them. We move from judgment and defense to curiosity and compassion. From there, the urge to move away or attack changes into willingness—or even eagerness—to go toward a resolution. Because of the neural circuitry we've built, there's time for this whole process to unfold before the next fighting words come out of our mouths.

And some days those words *will* come out anyway, deepening the upset. Fortunately, it is never too late to go back and repair wounds. The one thing that is necessary is that both people are willing to do it. I have been so disappointed at times when I have been yearning to make a repair, but my friend or partner or parent just couldn't do it. Honestly, it brings on a lot of grief because it is such a familiar pattern in my life. It is also a time I can turn to my anchors, to my therapist and trusted friends, to express the anger and deep sadness so that it doesn't become another whirlpool of unhealed pain. Thank heavens for this ever-growing circle of safe support.

THE BIG PICTURE OF HEALING

The paradox I have been shown through the work I'm doing is that any true awakening I have personally experienced is due to the fact that I have had enough support to move inward and downward. That may sound strange because we might think of awakening as rising—that if we evolve we move upward—but what I have learned is that it is when we move deeper into our own inner world, through our body, that we are creating the space that allows us to expand our awareness and take in what we need to heal.

Recovery never moves in a straight line, as much as our left hemispheres would like that to be the path. Instead, it is more like a wave as we drop down into the painful places over and over. As we touch the deep places inside, we plunge into the sensations again and again. Then we come back up to daily life, allowing the newly met parts of ourselves to integrate before we enter this world of implicit pain and fear again.

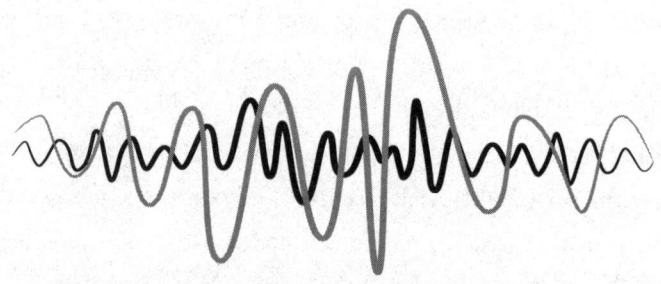

The image above shows the movement of two people's nervous systems, with the lighter line being the one experiencing an implicit memory and the darker line the person who is holding the safe space. This anchoring person resonates with us but is steady enough to hold their own experience and our experience without judgment or dysregulation. When it is time to drop down again into the traumatic memories, they remind us that this is the next step in healing and not some form of backsliding. Their ability to hold space and be with us helps ground us to stay present while the more intense experiences surface.

The healing journey can sometimes feel so confusing because it doesn't follow a straight path even when we are making progress.

Each time we drop into and hold our wounded selves with compassion and warmth, we come out of that painful place healthier and less burdened by our trauma. But at certain low points, we lose sight of the progression taking place in our healing. It can feel like every time we ascend a little, we're suddenly back at ground zero. This is because when our implicit wounds and sensations are fully reawakened, they rise to the surface and take over our whole perceptual reality. In those moments, it's hard to remember that the awakening implicit reality feels as though it is happening right now even though it is from the past. Reexperiencing pain so intensely can make us believe we are not moving at all. A feeling of "here I am again" can take over. This is when we need to lean into our anchors, who can see the bigger picture. They provide reassurance that we are touching all the necessary wounds, and that they are right by our side to help hold it all.

My clients often want to know how long this will go on. Believe me, I get it. As we are moving through the suffering, it can be quite scary and uncomfortable not to have a left-shifted map planned out for our healing. We want to know all the details—the when, where, why, and how. But this process has its own inner logic and movement that isn't accessible to our thinking minds. It's about allowing the memories to surface in an environment of deep safety and support according to the inner wisdom that guides everything to unfold in its own time.

If you have needed to protect yourself for decades from the wounds that are surfacing, there might be quite a lot of intense feelings to be experienced. It's impossible to know what will unfold. Because I had developed such reliance on work to protect me from profound wounds, I needed to lean in to my anchors and find a therapist to hold me until I felt safe enough to encounter my inner world. I knew I had to keep showing up to therapy even when I wasn't sure what was happening, to give my protectors room to soften. Bit by bit, I could feel the inner space expanding as I made room for that descent again and again. I felt major shifts, and so—even amidst the really hard stuff—I knew I was healing. Having this knowledge in the science of healing gave me comfort during my harder periods. That's what I want for you—to allow for your unique unfolding in your own, well-accompanied healing journey.

None of us ever arrive at a final destination, but there are some beautiful changes that reliably happen along the way. In our last chapter, we're going to spend some time with the new patterns of life that await us as we continue with this beautiful work.

CHAPTER 9

REACHING YOUR SAFE HARBOR

This last chapter is a celebration of the path we've walked together in this book. As the warm and safe haven we've developed within and around us expands, it is my hope that you are experiencing some beautiful changes in your life. Each of you will be having unique experiences on the way to healing your attachment wounds. Most of us begin this work with similar questions. "How long will it take?" (I remember asking my therapist, Jo, that when we began.) "When will I not have to do all this inner exploration anymore, and be able to just get on with my life?" I get it. In order to try and answer these questions, I will share what my own experience of digging deep inside myself these past five years has been.

At this stage of my life, I can't imagine *not* continuing to be in relationship with my inner world in this way. There is such sweetness in the connection between my Little Me and my adult self. Because of all the healing we have done, I don't get overwhelmed by her pain and fear the same way I did in the beginning. Instead, as an old memory emerges, she comes to me more quietly. First, I feel her approaching me through sensations in my body, gently asking me to listen and care for her and to stay with her until she is able to join me in my present moment. I can do that now.

My relationship with my Little Me is essential, but so, too, is my relationship with the community of caring anchors who have become woven into my daily life. Because of the depths of my wounds, it has also been vital for me to have a therapist who has held me without judgment or agenda. I have internalized her so deeply that she will always be my inner companion. Equally important are the friends who have been willing to go deep with me. Our intimacy has grown to become an oasis of safety for all of us. The life-giving experience of being deeply heard and, in turn, deeply hearing these dear people in my life has given me so much hope and internal steadiness. These are the fruits of my growing sense of inner safety.

Whether we believe we *need* it or not, living in heartfelt connection with others brings so much nourishment, depth, and meaning into our lives. It is also intrinsic to who we are as human beings. I often find myself whispering Stephen Porges's wise words to myself: "Connection is a biological imperative." It is a reminder for me that we are meant to receive others and to be received. And reminding ourselves that we *do* need the warm sanctuary of our relationships is especially important now, as our collective traumatic experiences are all around us. Our planet is in crisis. We face cultural polarization at an unprecedented level. Our surgeon general spoke of a crisis of loneliness that is harming our physical, mental, emotional, and relational health. Even with a great deal of healing, we continue to need each other to move through these perilous times.

The work we have been engaged with in this book has the potential to heal *intergenerational* patterns. We carry not only our own personal wounds, but the pain and adaptations that the pioneers of the science of epigenetics tell us go as far back as fourteen generations. Imagine that your great-great-great-grandmother's fear and her way of dealing with that fear have become part of you. My father's parents were Holocaust survivors, and I am sure that terror has been passed down, amplifying the frightening experiences I've had in my lifetime. My mother struggles with her own intergenerational history of abandonment. In my parents' young lives, people didn't know much about how trauma flows like a powerful river from generation to generation. People who struggled emotionally were simply thought to be flawed, and the need for therapy was stigmatized. Instead of being supported, my parents' generation was pushed to survive and work hard, dealing with their pain and fear through the inner protections of addiction and avoidance.

As we have experienced, we have internalized our parents in profound ways, and this gives us the possibility of providing healing for the parts of them that we carry in our inner world. Later in my healing journey, after I worked through many of my own wounds, I was ready to also touch and sift through my father's highly traumatized inner landscape, a world I had internalized as part of my inner community. Encountering the terrified and lonely little one inside him, I could not only understand but also feel why he had little to no capacity to show up for me in any other way than financially. I could sense why he often needed to numb his feelings and be swept away in his relationships to keep from drowning in the torment his parents had experienced. It is still true that his abandonment hurt me profoundly, and as I have shared in this book, influenced my romantic choices. But the internal healing I have experienced lets me see him with compassionate eyes now. It is as though a much larger window has opened inside me so I can hold both the truth of my losses and a deep, felt sense of knowing that this was the best my father had to offer me. Our relationship is better now because my expectations of him are tempered by my experience and understanding of his inner world. Though this turbulence is largely unhealed in him, I am able to hold space for him through my own healing.

Healing goes something like this. If our parents weren't able to be present with us, we are left with the equivalent of raw wounds inside. We find ways to keep these hurting places from making our lives completely impossible, but the protective strategies we develop ultimately change the way we see the world. They also impact who we draw toward us and how we relate to them in relationship. Then, if we are lucky, a few trusted people come along who provide safe haven for us so we can become vulnerable enough for our inner protectors to step aside and bring this grief, fear, and pain into the light, where our anchors, both internal and external, meet it with the care that can soothe our pain. Over days, months, sometimes years, we are received enough that the felt sense in our bodies shifts in the direction of feeling safe, welcomed, loved, and tended. Then, like any wound that has healed, a scar remains. This scar makes us stronger than we were, and yet it also serves as a tender reminder that these things happened to us and that we must always keep searching for and maintaining safety in our lives. This is how the wound becomes the gift.

◎

CULTIVATING COMPASSION

As we approach the end of our journey together, I would like to take some time to reflect more deeply on what happens when we heal. What does it actually look like? As you read the following italicized statements about these markers of true healing, perhaps you can sense how you are relating now to any wounds that are still in the process of healing or any injuries that have become scars. Your journal and your internal and external anchors might like to hear about it as well. Then a few months or years from now, you can return here and see how it has continued to unfold for you.

Walking this path tends to expand our compassion for others and ourselves, and then for the world at large.

One of the things that has supported me in developing compassion is learning something about relational neuroscience. How we are built for caring relationships and for kindness toward one another. How our wounds, particularly the implicit memories of early attachment, shape the way we see and treat each other. How much these patterns can change when our early losses are met with nonjudgmental care that supplies what we missed as children. How compassion grows naturally as we are received in this way so that we are able to receive others, even those who have hurt us, more generously. I am so grateful this has happened with my parents.

My own process has helped me support my clients as well. I've worked with Andrew for about three years now. He came in telling me that his hatred and fear of his older brother was disturbing his relationship with his wife. He clearly loved her deeply and felt so sad that this piece of "ancient history" was hurting her and them. When they met, Andrew was estranged from his family, so Stella never felt the panic or the hard, cold place inside him that could rise up to protect him from fully feeling the effects of the traumas he had experienced at the hands of his only sibling, Dillon, who was ten years older than Andrew. Now, with both their parents aging poorly, he was being called on to help with their care. There was no way of avoiding Dillon, so the powerful protectors were often awake inside Andrew.

Andrew told me about the daily violence he'd experienced at the hands of his adopted brother. Both of their parents had to work two jobs to make ends meet, so these boys were left alone together from the time Andrew was about five. Before being adopted at five, Dillon had lived in a home in which he'd been assaulted since infancy. Andrew told me that he intellectually understood why Dillon hurt him, but that didn't do anything to change what happened inside him at the thought of spending time with his brother.

We decided to bring Stella in to relieve her fears about what was happening to her husband and to become a team on behalf of the terrified little boy inside Andrew. Talking about implicit memory and the protectors we develop to shield ourselves from drowning in these old wounds helped ease her feeling that she was losing her husband.

After that, Stella often sat with us, making it safer for Andrew to approach these terrifying memories. We spent time with Andrew's little boy inside, and then he was ready to work with his internalized Dillon. Even though Andrew knew his brother's history, it was an entirely different experience to stand in Dillon's shoes internally and experience the terror and torment that caused him to furiously lash out at his younger brother. Andrew felt how his birth had been such a tragedy for Dillon, who legitimately needed more attention than his overworked parents could give. And he felt how the violence in Dillon's birth family had simply flowed downstream to him.

Stella and I watched as compassion for his brother developed over the weeks and months. Dillon had gotten his own help and was a different person as an adult. He had wanted to reunite with Andrew but also understood that his kid brother had every reason to avoid him. Now, as Andrew emerged from the burden of unhealed traumas, he could experience Dillon as the adult he had become rather than feeling him as the violent teenager he had been. Even if his brother hadn't been healing from his own wounds, Andrew's relationship with him would have been very different because he now carried his own sense of inner safety with him.

We don't have to use any specific techniques to generate compassion. It arises slowly and naturally from the work we do with our inner communities.

We find ourselves being more curious than judgmental when we see people doing unkind or hurtful things.

Instead of automatically thinking, *What a jerk!*, we begin to ask, "How must they be hurting inside to leave their natural human impulse to care in favor of such protection?" Often when an angry driver flips me the bird or otherwise acts aggressively, inside I think there is a strong possibility that a good deal of sadness lies beneath all that road rage. As I healed, rather than being swallowed up in the pain of my mother's inability to be with me, I found room inside myself to pause and wonder about the causes for this abandonment. Who had left her? Even if I didn't fully know the answer, just the question softened our relationship.

We will always have left hemispheres that have a tendency to judge others and ourselves, but as we heal, we usually begin to be able to catch ourselves in the act more often. The next step is to be gentle with our judging parts. As I got more attuned to how the harsh critic in me was trying to keep me in line, I became more able to help others with this miserable tendency.

Mitchell came to see me because he was having debilitating headaches that didn't seem to have a physical cause. As we explored what seemed to bring them on, he noticed that his right temple began to ache just about every time a voice in his head said to him, "Shut up and don't rock the boat, you idiot!"

I asked whose voice that was, and he immediately said, "Mine."

As we listened some more to the voice, implicit memories from early childhood began to come to the surface. He saw his parents' frowning faces when, in his natural exuberance, he would interrupt the adults talking when they had company. Or when he rushed toward something that fascinated him without checking to see if it was okay. He felt like he lost their love just by being a curious, excited, delighted kid. So his wise inner world developed a protector who did his best to keep him in line so as not to risk further relational losses, whether he was at work or at home. And now the pain in his head was trying to get his attention so that someone would come along to rescue the little boy whose enthusiasms were being stifled.

As we felt our way into the world of this protector, it was easy to feel gratitude for the way he tried to make sure Mitchell wouldn't lose precious connections again. As we smiled gently with the little one inside, enjoying his delight and supporting the curiosity he had needed to put aside, the critical protector's voice got quiet.

Because we aren't devoting all of our energy to protecting ourselves from the pain in our inner world, we can be more attuned to our empathic connection with our fellow humans.

I had been in so much terror when my partner would pull away from me, all I could do was devote my full attention to protecting myself, first by doing everything possible to get him back, then by getting angry with him, and finally by collapsing into despair. Even if I had thought about the pain he might be in, I didn't have the emotional energy to be concerned about him. But as my Little Me got the care she needed, I found my attention to the wounds driving his behavior coming into my awareness with greater clarity. And this involved so much more than just an increased ability to absorb more information about my partner's situation and to feel more understanding of his experience. I had the bandwidth now to feel into his inner world—a natural ability we all have—and this resonance informed my empathy for him. Even though my partner wasn't receptive to my care because it would have made him vulnerable in ways he wasn't ready to embrace, the inner sense of standing next to him with empathy felt so much better to me.

I have seen this same shift in just about everyone I've worked with. When the pain and fear in our inner world no longer commands our full attention, our inborn capacity for empathy grows naturally. When we are relieved of the need to have so much protection, we have the safety and energy to become conscious of the feelings of others. Suffering is universal. When we begin to expansively feel part of the community of our fellow humans, even the pain and fear we are all experiencing has meaning. We are in this together, and that makes all the difference.

When we make mistakes, instead of being hard on ourselves, we move in the direction of comfort with our humanness and seek to offer the best repair we can.

This one is especially important because it requires us to work with the shame we carry inside ourselves in order to come to a place where the left-hemisphere standards of perfection, performance, and achievement no longer mean much to us. It is only after we have shed our deep shame that we can have more compassion for ourselves.

Like any child who has experienced abandonment, I carried a lot of shame into adulthood. I felt I would be loved only if I was as close to perfect as possible. This left me in survival mode, anxious all the time, and desperate to keep the shame I felt from surfacing. The broad acceptance I felt from my anchors, no matter how "imperfect" I might be, is gradually repairing the humiliating sense of never being good enough. Now, if I say or do something that causes someone else distress, I can much more easily remember that I'm only human and find joy in seeking repair. Healing brings humility. And humility brings the possibility of ever-deepening connections.

I have not met anyone—friends or clients or fellow therapists—who doesn't have some experience of shame. Our bodies tell us this truth through our impulse to curl up in a ball and disappear when someone criticizes us. It doesn't even have to come at us in words. Everyone has ways of conveying their displeasure with a look or tone of voice. If we endured shaming as a child, it may now all happen internally, as it did for Mitchell, shutting him down. The antidote to shame is full acceptance of ourselves—even of the parts we feel the most ashamed of. Warm curiosity about their origin instead of dislike or avoidance begins to move us away from the pervasive left-hemisphere push to be perfect, ashamed of anything anyone might deem *less*. The relief of just accepting that we are flawed, yet resilient and honest humans together is at the heart of mental and emotional well-being.

As we spend more time in a state of safety, we are more open to experiences of beauty, wonder, and awe.

Each of us may experience this increased sense of aliveness differently. As my felt sense of safety grew and grew, everything in my life became more vivid, as though the colors and sounds were more brilliant. I live near the ocean and the ever-shifting way it reflects the light gives me a sense of awe every day. Nature seems to dance more—be it in the movement of the clouds hovering above the water or the gentle waves hitting the shore that I view as I take my daily walks with my dog. I feel more and more enchanted by the place I live and the world at large. The word that comes to me about these experiences is *sacred*. It now feels to me as if there is something bigger than all of us holding us in its gracious arms. I truly don't believe that there was room for this change in my perspective until the embodied implicit memories of pain and fear began to heal.

So many of my clients over the years have found themselves spontaneously drawn to some deeply meaningful path that one could call spiritual as they healed. Each emergence was unique. Genevieve became a wildlife photographer and advocate, engaging in a heartfelt way with the beautiful creatures whose images she captured with her camera. Barney moved from a church that had the feeling of God as judge to one whose pastor's presence reminded him that God is love. Leanna, eighty-one when I first met her, had never gardened in her life but became a dedicated gardener, communing with the plants she cultivated. David found meaning joining a band and started to let his passion for creating music with others fill him up. James discovered he liked to write poetry, and Samantha spent many Saturdays serving food and laughter to homeless teenagers. What they all have in common is a sense of the meaningfulness of life. As an added bonus, research tells us that meaning and companionship are what make for a joyous (and healthier) old age.

The world continues to be the world, but with healing, there is more resilience in challenging times.

Before these five past years of healing work, it felt like my inner world could crumble easily in the face of any kind of emotional hardship. The worst part was difficulties in my primary relationship because that is where my implicit wounds were touched most deeply and most often. The threat of abandonment was so great that all my attention had to be focused right there. When I began this healing work, I made the decision not to get right back into a romantic relationship. That gave me the time to focus on the implicit traumas that had so deeply affected my choice of a primary relationship.

In some ways, I was deeply lonely during that time, but that was gradually being alleviated as I spent more time with my anchors. But of course we couldn't always be together. This gave me the opportunity to see what happened inside me when one of those precious people wasn't available right when I needed them. In the early days, I felt a good deal of panic and terror arising in my body. It was very uncomfortable to feel these sensations and emotions on my own, even for the few hours it took until one of my anchors was available again to provide a much-needed disconfirming experience through their ongoing love and care. Now, with five years of healing inside me, I can feel how much more expansive my inner world is when no one is immediately available. I may feel some twinges of fear and sadness, but I can turn to my internalized anchors and to the general sense of trust and safety inside. Breathing a little deeper, I can settle and attend to whatever is next. More and more, that baseline state of safety is available for balance and steadiness.

As all the changes begin to show themselves, sometimes unexpectedly, our natural response is often gratitude for the process and for those who are with us along this healing path.

I have been stunned by the way gratitude simply wells up in my chest these days. Neuroscience researchers tell us that the neurotransmitters dopamine and serotonin are released when we feel grateful. Especially when that feeling comes up spontaneously. Dopamine fuels our delighted movement toward who and what fascinates us, and serotonin supports our ability to feel fulfillment and ease. You may be able to sense this if you call to mind and heart a time when gratitude swept over you. What happens in your body—your belly, your chest, your muscles, your breathing? Just let yourself settle into that feeling, knowing your whole physiology is being soaked in the neurochemicals arising from the hard work you have been willing to do.

Over the years, I've come to deeply appreciate our bodies' inherent movement toward healing once the needed support arrives. A lot of my gratitude also comes from feeling myself surrounded, internally and externally, by this anchoring community of people who care, who repair, and who humbly understand the meaning in going down this road together.

Before we part, I want to share perhaps one of the most important things I've learned on my journey. *No one experiences these beautiful states all the time.* Remember the picture in chapter 8 of the nervous systems that resemble waves dropping us into implicit memories and then bringing us up for integration? That doesn't just happen when we are in the deepest parts of our healing time. That is life itself. After the wounds that affect us most deeply heal and we are finding our way to a much more fulfilling life, new experiences will still sometimes touch and wake up unhealed places. A client I hadn't seen in a while called me last week to tell me about her mother's dementia diagnosis and how it was touching her. We'll be meeting for a while again, as this monumental event is waking up further layers of her childhood experience. She is also in a major life transition: she and her sister are preparing to become the matriarchs of their family. It is my privilege to accompany her.

Because we are only (and wonderfully) human, we will also have times when we hurt one another in this moment. At no point in our lives will we stop being the tender and imperfect people that we are. We will make mistakes. People will misunderstand us. Once we give up on perfection, we can settle into the practice of rupture and repair, expecting to wound and be wounded at times, all the while cultivating the beautiful capacity to offer and receive heartfelt working-through and reconnection.

And then there are simply the conditions of living on this planet—conditions that include the most poignant beauty and deepest joys side by side with frightening and tragic events of all sorts. What is so different for us now is that at these hard moments, we are part of a community of care in which we surround and hold one another, repair the ruptured places, and find safety in the midst of it all.

Additional Information About Our Embodied Brains

For some of us, having more information can help us deepen into awareness of the various ways our remarkable brains are doing their best to help us thrive every day. If you feel drawn to learn more about our neural pathways, please honor that sense. For you, the practices that are sprinkled throughout the book may come more alive with the benefit of this knowledge. For others, the lived experiences I have been offering in the body of the book may feel complete on their own. Reading more may seem like a distraction. If that is the case, feel free to skip this part and simply keep practicing. In the following pages, we'll visit with Stephen Porges, Iain McGilchrist, Marco Iacoboni, James Coan, Bruce Ecker, and Lucia Capacchione. You can pick and choose which ones you want to sample.

STEPHEN PORGES AND POLYVAGAL THEORY

When Stephen Porges was a teenager, he felt socially awkward (as many of us do), but he noticed that when he played his clarinet, he felt calmer and more open to being with people. Being a curious person by nature, he began to wonder why that was. This started him down the path of research that led to what he calls the polyvagal theory of the autonomic nervous system (ANS for short). For Porges, there was no better place to begin than with his own experience.

Our autonomic nervous system is made up of long, wandering neural pathways that touch many of our internal organs. It responds to our neuroception of being safe, not-safe-but-I-can-do-something-to-protect-myself, or helpless. Neuroception refers to our embodied awareness of our internal state that hasn't yet become conscious.

If I am experiencing a neuroception of safety, the branch of the ANS that becomes active is called the *ventral vagal parasympathetic*, or *ventral* for short. When my neuroception shifts to danger but I feel I could do something like fight or flee, it is the sympathetic branch that takes over. And when things become more dangerous to the point that I feel helpless, leading to the sense that I might die, then the dorsal vagal parasympathetic (dorsal for short) takes the lead. All of these changes are adaptive to give us the best chance of survival. In other words, one is not better than the other.

These neuroceptions are based on three conditions: which implicit memories are awake inside me, what is coming toward me from the outside world, and who is or isn't with me right now. Any of us might be walking down the street feeling safe, enjoying the day, with or without a companion. When that is our neuroception, ventral comes alive in us. Our system prefers ventral (whose other name is the social engagement system) because it supports being in warm relationship with others. Since connection is a biological imperative, it makes sense that ventral is what our system prefers.

Lots of lovely things happen physiologically that support our connection with others when we are in ventral. A small muscle near our inner ear tightens so that we can focus on what others are saying. They will feel it, too, because their neuroceptive activity is on the lookout for those who can truly listen. Our vocal cords are also affected by being in ventral, giving our voice a particular quality that lets others sense our ANS status and invites them to come closer. We can't fake ventral, and when we try, our voice quality gives us away. In ventral, our bodies and faces become more responsive and animated, and even the area around our eyes becomes more relaxed in ways that people pick up below conscious awareness. We are a walking invitation to all those around us to come close and engage.

It's also true that we could be walking along feeling safe and easy when all of a sudden we begin to feel afraid, even though nothing has changed on the outside. Most likely, we have had an implicit awakening of a memory containing fear, and the sensations from that memory are rippling through our body's system, telling us there is danger even though the outside remains safe. If I'm walking with a trustworthy friend, I can share this, and if they listen and don't tell me I'm wrong or try to fix it, my system can often settle because I am heard. If I'm walking alone or with a person who needs to change how I'm feeling, the inner experience often intensifies because I'm not heard.

Initially, though, when I begin to feel afraid, the sympathetic branch of my ANS adaptively takes precedence because it gives me the best chance to protect myself from what is scaring me. My system needs to shift in ways that support fighting or fleeing. These two ways of being with fear can take many forms, but essentially it means engaging with the danger in some active way because my system believes it can protect itself.

Lots of things happen when the sympathetic takes over in response to fear, regardless of its source. Most important, we adaptively shift away from focusing on connection with others to attend to the source of threat. Knowing this, if I'm talking with someone and I feel them shift away from attending to what I'm saying, I might think, *I wonder what scared them?* rather than, *What a jerk!* We also need to keep in mind that they may have no idea what just happened because the shift into a neuroception of danger often happens outside of conscious awareness. In addition to this narrowing of focus, our voice quality changes to convey urgency in its tone (a signal to others that danger is near), the area around our eyes goes from relaxed to tense, the fluidity of our body gives way to tension, and that little muscle near our inner ear relaxes to take in a broader range of sounds—which means we can no longer attend as closely to what another person is saying. All of this telegraphs itself to the neuroception of whomever is with us, influencing them to join us in a sympathetically activated state. The intent is safety for both people, but when the person who is afraid is responding to an inner awakening rather than a current danger, it can be confusing for the other person. However, if our companion has gone into a frightened state, we can trust that something very real and adaptive is happening for them whether it is because of outside events or something waking up inside.

We might also be walking down the street, easy with the beauty of the day, when we suddenly feel weak in the knees, with our mind becoming foggy. This is the leading edge of the third ANS state, called the *dorsal vagal parasympathetic*. It comes to our rescue when we have a neuroception of helplessness because of an inner awakening or something coming toward us in the outside world. There can be a quality of terror that brings us close to collapse, although experiences of shame and humiliation also are right at the edge of dorsal. If you pause for a moment to remember a time you felt shamed by someone's judgment, you may be able to feel the withdrawal, the need to hide and disappear. That sense of collapsing is the embodied signature of the onset of dorsal.

If we have experienced terror as children, the implicit memories holding that experience will also carry the felt sense of dorsal. It is just about 180 degrees opposite of sympathetic. Everything in our system slows down—heart rate, breathing, blood flow, muscle tension. Our faces become pale. Our eyes begin to look more and more vacant as we become less conscious of the outside world. We are seeking a safe place inside, a kind of hibernation until the extreme danger passes. Our body releases analgesic compounds so that if we were about to be hurt, we would hurt less. Such good care is being taken in these extreme circumstances. Through his insightful research, Porges reminds us that we are conserving our metabolic resources for a time when we can safely become active again. It is an inner state that is seeking to save our lives when the inner or outer danger feels most threatening.

As we heal, our neuroception of safety grows in our inner world. As our circle of caring others expands, we feel more settled internally and externally because we have companions who we trust can be with us—and us with them. Then when the world is challenging, we can find refuge and care in the sanctuary within while holding hands in the outside world.

◎

IAIN McGILCHRIST AND THE TWO HEMISPHERES OF OUR BRAINS

Iain McGilchrist was a student of literature and found that as he proceeded in his studies, he became increasingly distressed physically. There was an ever-increasing insistence that he analyze the poetry he was reading. For him, this amounted to dismembering these enchanting creations rather than allowing them to simply be received in their fullness. He found that this practice of dismemberment made him physically ill and began to wonder about what was happening in his brain.

Decades studying the two hemispheres of the brain began to yield some answers. We may have heard it said that the left hemisphere is for logic and the right for creativity, but in reality, both hemispheres of the brain fire all the time. Instead, the evidence

McGilchrist was uncovering suggested that each hemisphere of the brain sees and experiences the world differently, like looking through two different lenses. How we attend to the world determines which of the perspectives we experience at any given moment.

The way the two hemispheres are wired differently helps to explain this. Our neocortex is made up of columns of neurons, like silos. On the left, these silos are mostly isolated from each other. On the right, the silos are strongly intertwined with each other, constantly exchanging information. The right gives a felt sense of the whole. The left takes information, breaks it into bits, and categorizes it in the individual silos. For example, let's say I've encoded a memory of being in the redwood forest in California when I was a teenager. My right hemisphere will remember the felt sense of that particular trip to the woods, including the scent, the deep green of the canopy and the rich red-brown of the trunks, the towering immensity of these remarkable specimens, along with my emotional response to all of this. When the right hemisphere hands the memory off to the left, each bit of information becomes less personal and more factual and objective. We no longer have the experience of being in relationship with these magnificent trees. They are just objects without particular meaning. We consider them at arm's length, without as much personal investment.

Neither way of experiencing or remembering is right or wrong. Ideally in our relationships, the two work together, with the right relational hemisphere taking the lead and the left organizational hemisphere providing support. Unfortunately, it isn't that way in the developed Western world. The left has achieved dominance, and this has enormous consequences. It means our culture encourages us to believe that tasks are more important than relationships. That achieving something prestigious is more important than doing something meaningful. And it leaves us believing (mostly outside conscious awareness) that we are utterly alone even when there are people around. We can't help but feel that self-reliance, self-regulation, and individual success are what's most essential. Because the left hemisphere objectifies everything, even people, there's no sense of safe companionship and trust from others.

Why do these hemispheric differences matter as we are on this healing journey? We store the implicit experience of trauma in our right hemispheres and our bodies. Another way to say this is that we are in relationship with our trauma when we are attending with the right. When the burden is more than we can bear, one way of protecting ourselves is to shift into our left hemispheres, because this helps us dissociate from the pain while minimizing the importance of our traumatic experience. While this numbs the pain of experiencing the embodied trauma that is alive in our right hemisphere, it comes at great cost.

As much as our right hemisphere exposes us to our emotional wounds, it is also where we connect with others in safe, warm ways. And this is the key to the healing path we're walking here. As we are able to move toward people who can hold a safe enough space, we are gradually able to leave our left-hemisphere hideout and encounter the reality of our earlier experience in the embodied right. These trusted companions bring the disconfirming experiences (see Bruce Ecker on page 263) that mend the torn places inside. Gradually our right hemispheres become sanctuaries of safety and we are able to deepen our connections with those around us. The right and left hemispheres are able to hold hands and support our increasingly compassionate, meaningful, and creative life.

⊚

MARCO IACOBONI AND HOW WE "LIVE WITHIN EACH OTHER"

There's a lovely story about how mirror neurons were first discovered in the brains of primates—by accident. A macaque monkey was wired up so that Giacomo Rizzolatti and his researchers could look at activity in certain parts of the monkey's brain. A graduate student walked into the lab eating an ice cream cone and noticed that the monkey's brain lit up as though he were holding and eating the treat himself. At first the researchers thought there had been an error, but when they were able to repeat the activity, they realized they had discovered a new kind of neuron, one that linked the experience of human and monkey. They called them *mirror neurons*.

After hearing about these remarkable brain cells, Marco Iacoboni began to wonder if human brains have something similar. The answer is yes. Like everything else in our neural universe, mirror neurons don't do their work alone but are integrated with what are called the *resonance circuits* in various parts of our brains. They are activated by the presence of others. If we see someone looking sad, the resonance circuitry in our brain activates for sadness, and there is a good chance we will feel empathy for them. The other possibility is that our own sadness is so deep that this resonance brings surges of grief rather than empathy. In either case, we experience an emotional reaction that's strong and authentic.

These reactions are more than fleeting. We also encode the presence of the person whose sadness we encountered. We take in their emotional and bodily state as well as their intention toward us (if they're noticing us). That might be worth reading a second and third time. You may begin to sense that that's a lot of important information/experience about another person that comes to live inside us—and the more long-standing the relationship, the larger the effect on us.

If I am with you physically, and your belly and muscles are relaxed as you are feeling welcomed by me, I am taking in your experience side by side with my own, mostly below the level of conscious awareness. At the same time, a certain part of my neural equipment senses whether your intention is to help or to harm me. At the same time, I am encoding what you look like, sound like, perhaps what you smell like, and (if I'm a baby nibbling on your fingers) what you taste like. In other words, my amazing brain is making the part of you who is with me right then part of me. The felt sense and tangible experience of our relationship is now part of my inner world. As Marco Iacoboni says, "We live within each other." Throughout our lives, we continue to develop a vast *inner community* of relationships, some small and some powerfully dominant inside.

Because connection is a biological imperative, this ability to keep others with us is of enormous significance. However, we also internalize parts of others who have harmed us. This can seem daunting, but keeping them close may also be of tremendous importance to our ability to heal. Resolving relational pain is one of the most essential parts of the mending from trauma. The traumatic events themselves require attention, but it is often the experiences of betrayal, abandonment, and lack of protection that cause the deepest wounds. Because we carry the presence of these individuals within us, because they are part of our neurobiology, we can find healing with them internally when there is no hope of resolution with the person on the outside.

Neither of my parents have done the kind of work that would allow us to repair together, but because I have been able to come into contact with them in my inner world, I am developing compassion for the wounds in them that led to them harming me. At the same time, I can provide safety and comfort for those internalized parts of them who were wounded so that there is true resolution within me. This can sound like a mysterious process, but once we have the support to go deeply into our inner community, we become more profoundly aware of how accompanied we are and how possible deep healing is.

JAMES COAN AND SOCIAL BASELINE THEORY

James Coan is an expert in the neurobiology of attachment and has studied how the presence of a safe person affects our experience of pain or difficulty with a task. In one of many experiments on the nature of close connections, researchers place a person alone at the bottom of a hill and ask them to estimate the steepness of the hill. Then they do the same thing, this time with a friend accompanying them. Consistently, the hill looks less steep in the company of a familiar person. Regardless of the task, it feels less daunting when someone familiar is right there. Perhaps you've experienced this yourself—whether relying on a gym buddy or prepping for a big exam with a group of fellow students rather than on your own.

A second piece of research finds Coan and his colleagues putting a person in a scanner under three conditions: alone, with a stranger holding their hand, and with a trusted beloved holding their hand. In the scanner, he shows them either a red X to indicate that there is a 20 percent chance of them receiving a shock or a blue circle to indicate that they are safe. Several things happen. When the possibility of the shock is there but hasn't arrived, anticipatory discomfort is reduced most when the safe, familiar person is holding their hand. When the shock comes, the pain is less with a stranger's hand to hold and a lot less severe with a trusted person. Most interesting, when the target of the shock is the person outside the scanner, the person in the scanner responds to the threat of a shock as though the pain might happen to them, most strongly when the person outside is a trusted beloved. Coan says the person in the scanner is experiencing their beloved as themselves. Their sense of self has *expanded* to include this safe and familiar person.

In other words, we are meant to be neurobiologically entwined with safe others in ways that make tasks easier and pain less extreme while giving us an ongoing sense of companionship and support. He says that we have evolved to expect to find ourselves in a nest of familiar others, and anything less than that is a violation of what our systems need. If you and I are in a trusting relationship, when we meet each other at the door or hear each other's voices, we each settle a little bit inside. Life is better.

BRUCE ECKER AND THE HEALING OF IMPLICIT MEMORY

There is a recent field of research in relational neuroscience called *memory reconsolidation*. Exploring how implicit memory can change over time, Bruce Ecker and his colleagues discovered that there are two conditions necessary for the neural nets holding trauma to open and receive a new, transformative experience. The first is that the implicit memory must be awake in the body, meaning that the sensations and the emotions are actively being experienced. The second is that another safe and attuned person is bringing the embodied experience of what was needed at the time but not available. For instance, if we received little affection as a child and are feeling that loss in this moment, the presence of someone who clearly cares about us offers what we always needed. Bruce calls this a *disconfirming experience*. In these transformative moments, the neural net opens and at least two things happen. The first is that we internalize the person who is offering this experience. Instead of feeling alone with the trauma, we begin to feel *accompanied*. This is healing in and of itself. The second piece is that we *take in* the disconfirming experience, which begins to change the felt sense of the memory.

Let me give you an example. You are having a memory of being yelled at by your uncle, something that happened every time you saw him. As the memory awakens in your body, you feel your stomach quake and you begin to shake with fear. Your good friend is with you and feels an inner urge to protect you, to step between you and this uncle. It is the meeting of these two embodied experiences that opens the neural net to healing. Your friend's caring presence is felt by the younger part of you who is experiencing the memory. You are no longer alone with it. At the same time, you sense that your friend wants to protect you. This felt sense of safety begins to enter the neural net as well.

The research in memory reconsolidation tells us that about five hours later this neural net will close, carrying the new experience with it. If we have had the same kind of painful or frightening experience many times, we will likely need more than one disconfirming experience to resolve the trauma. Bit by bit, this stream of memories will carry more accompaniment and greater safety. The explicit memory doesn't change. It will always be true that he yelled at you. But the felt sense of the memory will move in the direction of warmth and safety. There may always be appropriate sadness, too, as you wish he had been a more loving presence, but this is the nontraumatic response of an increasingly compassionate, healing person.

Ecker tells us that there is no such thing as pathology. There is nothing "wrong" with us. We develop *protective strategies* because our system believes that being in contact with the pain and fear underneath would be more harmful to us than whatever difficulty the protection is causing. When we are accompanied, we combine our emotional resources with another person's, and that makes it possible for us to touch and heal the traumas that are too much for our system when we are on our own.

You may notice one thing as you read about these pioneers in relational neuroscience. They all come to the same conclusion. *We need each other and are meant to be safely together under all circumstances.*

LUCIA CAPACCHIONE AND NONDOMINANT HAND DRAWING

I wanted to include this remarkable woman here in appreciation for her work in making nondominant hand drawing known to the world. In 1988, she published a book, *The Power of Your Other Hand.* Neuroscience was telling us that our nondominant hand is connected to the part of our brain that holds our traumas. When we put a crayon or pastel in that hand (attending to what color feels just right) and simply allow the energy and impulse in our bodies to direct its movement, we can come into contact with these embodied and often very early memories that have no words. The expression of these impulses and being witnessed without judgment or agenda during the expression can be the very disconfirming experience that Bruce Ecker and his colleagues talk about. What emerges isn't a picture, but instead an energetic pattern held in the body—made visible.

After drawing, placing your hands on various parts of the picture can help you come into contact with what is being expressed.

It may also be felt as a gesture of comfort toward the parts of you that have offered the drawing. We often won't "know" the meaning of the image. What is before or beyond language is most often beyond rational understanding. Instead, we may have the sense of encountering something important.

A very small percentage of us may be wired so that the emotional part of our brain is connected to our dominant hand. If you try this practice and feel more connected to your inner world with your dominant hand, please follow your experience. It is the best teacher.

ACKNOWLEDGMENTS

When reflecting on the people who have helped me on this journey, I can't help but think of the core theme of this book. Its creation was possible only because of an abundance of support from remarkable individuals, each contributing in their unique and talented ways. It truly took a village, and for that, I am deeply grateful.

To my agent, Kathy Schneider, thank you for your guidance and belief in me. Sara Carder, your brilliance in helping me shape the concept of this book and refining my voice during the writing process has been invaluable—thank you for your insight and creativity. I am forever grateful to my mentor, Bonnie Badenoch, whose compassionate understanding of attachment and human behavior has profoundly shaped this book and continues to leave a lasting impact on my journey. Your guidance and influence on me inspired the creation of this manuscript. To my project manager and soul sister, Melissa Montalvo, you have been my rock through this process and beyond. I could not be more grateful for your support in my life and in our work together. My editor, Marian Lizzi, thank you for your meticulous attention to detail and your ability to refine the manuscript while deeply understanding its essence. I am also immensely grateful to my publishers and the entire team at Tarcher for helping bring this work into the world.

A heartfelt thank-you to Jo Hadlock-King, whose unwavering presence and support over the years have given me the safety to heal my youngest and most vulnerable parts. Your work has been a humbling gift and a transformative force in my life. To Alan Stevens, your boundless patience and friendship have been a cornerstone of my journey—I am so lucky to have you. Julia Newlin-Smith, thank you for being such a nurturing anchor. Your warmth and consistency have been a ray of sunshine since you came into my life. Andrea Karpel, you have been a wonderful anchor for me. Leionie Bryant, I love you. Esin Pinarli, thank you for being there for me during some of my hardest moments. You are a dear friend.

I am endlessly grateful to my entire team at the Relationship Institute of Palm Beach and Be Self-full. Licette Sangiovanni, thank you for being there all these years with such solid, consistent, and loyal support. To my behind-the-scenes team, Dario Fasolo and Karen McBride, thank you for your tireless work in helping to get this book out to the world and for your years of support.

To my parents, Karen Sakas and Fred Baum, thank you for loving me in the best ways you knew how and for supporting me as I openly share my personal story. Your acceptance and love mean the world to me. I love you both so much.

Finally, this book would not exist without the wisdom and contributions of so many people who have shaped the fields of attachment, trauma, and interpersonal neurobiology. Thank you to Stephen Porges, Iain McGilchrist, and countless other mentors and researchers whose groundbreaking work has inspired and informed this manuscript. To the clients I've had the privilege of working with over the years, your courage and resilience inspire me every day. You have taught me so much, and your stories are interwoven throughout these pages.

It is clear to me now that creating a book like this is not a solo endeavor. It requires a team of incredible individuals whose combined talents and support make it possible. To everyone mentioned here—and those who are not but remain close to my heart—thank you for being a part of this journey. I am forever grateful.

NOTES

Introduction

xiv **We are literally built to be in warm, receptive relationships:** Matthew D. Lieberman, *Social: Why Our Brains Are Wired to Connect* (New York: Crown Publishers, 2013), 3–6, 43–47.

xvi **Instead, according to McGilchrist:** Iain McGilchrist, *The Master and His Emissary: The Divided Brain and the Making of the Western World* (New Haven, CT: Yale University Press, 2009), 154, 300.

xx **As the brilliant American psychologist:** Stephen W. Porges, *The Pocket Guide to the Polyvagal Theory: The Transformative Power of Feeling Safe* (New York: W. W. Norton & Company, 2017), 5–8.

xxi **I will also introduce you to:** Patty Wipfler, "What Is a Listening Partnership?" Hand in Hand Parenting, last modified August 2016, accessed November 29, 2024, https://www.handinhandparenting.org/2016/08/listen-launch-post-what-is-a-listening-partnership/.

xxv **One of the most important is:** Daniel J. Siegel, *Mindsight: The New Science of Personal Transformation* (New York: Bantam Books, 2010), 27.

Chapter 1: The Power of Connection

5 **Relational neuroscience tells us:** Allan N. Schore, *Affect Regulation and the Origin of the Self: The Neurobiology of Emotional Development*, 2nd ed. (New York: Routledge, 2003), 37–40.

6 **Renowned psychiatrist and researcher:** Porges, *The Pocket Guide to the Polyvagal Theory*, 5–8.

6 **In the 1950s, researcher John Bowlby:** Saul Mcleod, "Bowlby's Attachment Theory," *Simply Psychology*, February 5, 2017, https://www.simplypsychology.org/bowlby.html.

7 **Earlier in this chapter:** Jude Cassidy and Phillip R. Shaver, "Attachment Theory and Research: Overview with Suggested Applications to Child De-

velopment," *Oxford Research Encyclopedia of Psychology*, published online August 31, 2021, accessed November 29, 2024, https://oxfordre.com/psychology/view/10.1093/acrefore/9780190236557.001.0001/acrefore-9780190236557-e-51; Amir Levine and Rachel Heller, *Attached: The New Science of Adult Attachment and How It Can Help You Find—and Keep—Love* (New York: TarcherParigee, 2010), 111–115.

8   **They aren't able to regularly offer:** Cassidy and Shaver, "Attachment Theory and Research," *Oxford Research Encyclopedia of Psychology*, published online August 31, 2021.

9   **In order to create distance:** Cassidy and Shaver, "Attachment Theory and Research."

9   **In an avoidant family:** Levine and Heller, *Attached*, 95–100.

10 **But the researchers noticed:** Mary Main and Erik Hesse, "Parents' Unresolved Traumatic Experiences Are Related to Infant Disorganized Attachment Status: Is Frightened and/or Frightening Parental Behavior the Linking Mechanism?" in *Attachment in the Preschool Years: Theory, Research, and Intervention*, edited by M. T. Greenberg, D. Cicchetti, and E. M. Cummings (Chicago: University of Chicago Press, 1990), 161–182.

12 **According to the polyvagal theory:** Porges, *The Pocket Guide to the Polyvagal Theory*, 5–8, 19–20.

12 **Stephen Porges has coined a phrase:** Stephen W. Porges, *The Polyvagal Theory: Neurophysiological Foundations of Emotions, Attachment, Communication, and Self-Regulation* (New York: W. W. Norton & Company, 2011), 11–13.

13 **Neuroception is made up of:** Porges, *The Polyvagal Theory*, 115–120.

14 **When we are having a neuroception of safety:** Porges, *The Polyvagal Theory*, 26–27, 121–125.

16 **In fact, research by neuroscientist Ed Tronick:** Edward Z. Tronick and Adriano Gianino, "Interactive Mismatch and Repair: Challenges to the Coping Infant," *Zero to Three* 6, no. 3 (1986): 1–6.

Chapter 2: Finding Your Anchors

22 **Neuroscience researcher Marco Iacoboni:** Marco Iacoboni, *Mirroring People: The New Science of How We Connect with Others* (New York: Farrar, Straus and Giroux, 2008), 5–10, 263–265.

39 **Rachel Naomi Remen, physician, author, and mystic:** Rachel Naomi Remen, *Kitchen Table Wisdom: Stories That Heal*, 10th Anniversary Edition (New York: Riverhead Books, 2006), 159–160.

41 **One of my mentors-at-a-distance, Iain McGilchrist:** Iain McGilchrist, *The Matter with Things: Our Brains, Our Delusions, and the Unmaking of the World* (London: Perspectiva Press, 2021), 131–203.

42   **Researcher James Coan and his colleagues explore:** James A. Coan, Hillary S. Schaefer, and Richard J. Davidson, "Lending a Hand: Social Regulation of the Neural Response to Threat," *Psychological Science* 17, no. 12 (2006): 1032–1039.

Chapter 3: Welcoming Your Inner Protectors

50   **Bonnie Badenoch's book *The Heart of Trauma*:** Bonnie Badenoch, *The Heart of Trauma: Healing the Embodied Brain in the Context of Relationships* (New York: W. W. Norton & Company, 2017), 160–182.

52   **Psychologist Barbara Fredrickson's research:** Barbara L. Fredrickson et al., "A Functional Genomic Perspective on Human Well-Being," *Proceedings of the National Academy of Sciences* 110, no. 33 (2013): 13684–13689, https://doi.org/10.1073/pnas.1305419110; Emily Esfahani Smith, "Meaning Is Healthier Than Happiness," *The Atlantic*, August 1, 2013, https://www.theatlantic.com/health/archive/2013/08/meaning-is-healthier-than-happiness/278250/.

52   **At least ten thousand years ago:** National Geographic Society, "Development of Agriculture," *National Geographic Education*, accessed November 29, 2024, https://education.nationalgeographic.org/resource/development-agriculture/; University of Cambridge, "From Foraging to Farming: The 10,000-Year Revolution," *University of Cambridge News*, accessed November 29, 2024, https://www.cam.ac.uk/research/news/from-foraging-to-farming-the-10000-year-revolution.

53   **The illuminating research of psychiatrist Iain McGilchrist:** McGilchrist, *The Master and His Emissary*, 154, 300.

53   **Through Stephen Porges's and Iain McGilchrist's research:** Porges, *The Polyvagal Theory*, 284–287; McGilchrist, *The Master and His Emissary*, 133–135.

70   **In her groundbreaking work, Brené Brown shares:** Brené Brown, *Daring Greatly: How the Courage to Be Vulnerable Transforms the Way We Live, Love, Parent, and Lead* (New York: Gotham Books, 2012), 33–34.

Chapter 4: The Eternally Present Past

79   **Our memories are held in multiple systems:** Sabine C. Koch, Thomas Fuchs, and Michela Summa, "Body Memory: An Integration," in *Body Memory, Metaphor, and Movement*, edited by Sabine C. Koch, Thomas Fuchs, and Michela Summa (Amsterdam: John Benjamins Publishing Company, 2012), 1–16; *Frontiers in Psychology* Editorial Board, "Mechanisms of Embodiment," *Frontiers in Psychology* 6 (2015): 1525, https://doi.org/10.3389/fpsyg.2015.01525.

79 **These embodied recollections are called** *implicit memories*: Bessel A. van der Kolk, *The Body Keeps the Score: Brain, Mind, and Body in the Healing of Trauma* (New York: Viking, 2014), 193–197; Daniel J. Siegel, *The Developing Mind: How Relationships and the Brain Interact to Shape Who We Are*, 2nd ed. (New York: Guilford Press, 2012), 150–153.

80 **Researcher Andreas Riener:** Andreas Riener, "Subliminal Persuasion and Its Potential for Driver Behavior Adaptation," *Advances in Human Aspects of Transportation* (2012): 223–229, https://www.academia.edu/2347691/Subliminal_Persuasion_and_Its_Potential_for_Driver_Behavior_Adaptation; *Encyclopaedia Britannica*, s.v. "Information Theory: Physiology," accessed November 29, 2024, https://www.britannica.com/science/information-theory/Physiology.

81 **When we are in the company of someone who can:** Kathy L. Kain and Stephen J. Terrell, *Nurturing Resilience: Helping Clients Move Forward from Developmental Trauma—An Integrative Somatic Approach* (Berkeley, CA: North Atlantic Books, 2018), 20–22.

84 **It is worth saying again:** Harville Hendrix and Helen LaKelly Hunt, *Getting the Love You Want: A Guide for Couples*, 3rd ed. (New York: St. Martin's Press, 2019), 1–3; Badenoch, *The Heart of Trauma*, 10–12.

86 **The sensations we experience:** Mugdha Tendulkar et al., "Clinical Potential of Sensory Neurites in the Heart and Their Role in Decision-Making," *Frontiers in Neuroscience* 17 (2024): 1308232, https://doi.org/10.3389/fnins.2023.1308232.

92 **Now let's spend some time with our belly:** Michael D. Gershon, *The Second Brain: A Groundbreaking New Understanding of Nervous Disorders of the Stomach and Intestine* (New York: HarperCollins, 1998), 15–20; Queensland Brain Institute, "Enteric Nervous System," accessed November 29, 2024, https://qbi.uq.edu.au/brain/brain-anatomy/peripheral-nervous-system/enteric-nervous-system.

97 **When these old traumatic memories wake up:** Bruce Ecker, Robin Ticic, and Laurel Hulley, *Unlocking the Emotional Brain: Eliminating Symptoms at Their Roots Using Memory Reconsolidation* (New York: Routledge, 2012), 1–3, 30–31.

Chapter 6: Healing the Patterns That Keep Us Stuck

143 **A longing for warm, safe relationships:** Lieberman, *Social*, 3–6, 43–47; Porges, *The Polyvagal Theory*, 284–289; Siegel, *Mindsight*, 17.

147 **It's just the beginning of the relationship:** Harvard Medical School, "Love and the Brain," *Harvard Medical School News*, accessed November 29, 2024, https://hms.harvard.edu/news-events/publications-archive/brain/love-brain.

Chapter 7: Knowing When to Stay—and When It's Time to Go

199   **Psychologists and others use the term** *borderline*: Adolph Stern, "Psycho-analytic Investigation of and Therapy in the Borderline Group of Neuroses," *The Psychoanalytic Quarterly* 7, no. 4 (1938): 467–489.

201   **Fortunately, in the late 1970s, Marsha Linehan:** Marsha M. Linehan, *Cognitive-Behavioral Treatment of Borderline Personality Disorder* (New York: Guilford Press, 1993), xiii, 3–7, 112–114.

Chapter 8: What Happens When We Heal?

220   **Because our traumas live in our bodies:** Bessel A. van der Kolk, *The Body Keeps the Score: Brain, Mind, and Body in the Healing of Trauma* (New York: Viking, 2014), 169–173, 185–189; National Cancer Institute, "Risk Factors: Chronic Inflammation," accessed December 1, 2024, https://www.cancer.gov/about-cancer/causes-prevention/risk/chronic-inflammation.

225   **Deep in our brains lie neural connections:** Cleveland Clinic, "Amygdala: What It Is and What It Controls," last modified October 12, 2022, accessed December 1, 2024, https://my.clevelandclinic.org/health/body/24894-amygdala.

225   **Near our amygdala:** Allan N. Schore, "Using Modern Attachment Theory to Guide Clinical Assessments of Early Attachment Relationships," in *The Healing Power of Emotion: Affective Neuroscience, Development & Clinical Practice*, edited by Diana Fosha, Daniel J. Siegel, and Marion F. Solomon (New York: W. W. Norton & Company, 2009), 112–114.

225   **If this kind of nurturing environment isn't available:** Allan N. Schore, *Affect Regulation and the Repair of the Self* (New York: W. W. Norton & Company, 2003), 90–95.

225   **These new links make pathways for the flow of:** Louis Cozolino, *The Neuroscience of Psychotherapy: Healing the Social Brain*, 3rd ed. (New York: W. W. Norton & Company, 2017), 65–70; Siegel, *Mindsight*, 45–48.

226   **Neuroscientists tell us:** Porges, *The Polyvagal Theory*, 284–289; Siegel, *Mindsight*, 20–25, 82–86.

230   **It feels wonderful when everything is rolling:** Edward Z. Tronick, *The Neurobehavioral and Social-Emotional Development of Infants and Children* (New York: W. W. Norton & Company, 2007), 15–20, 152–155.

Chapter 9: Reaching Your Safe Harbor

237   **We carry not only our own personal wounds:** Eva Jablonka and Gal Raz, "Transgenerational Epigenetic Inheritance: Prevalence, Mechanisms, and Implications for the Study of Heredity and Evolution." *The Quarterly Review of Biology* 84, no. 2 (2009): 131–176.

248 **Neuroscience researchers tell us that:** Madhuleena Roy Chowdhury, "The Neuroscience of Gratitude and Effects on the Brain," *PositivePsychol ogy.com*, last modified October 19, 2023, accessed December 1, 2024, https://positivepsychology.com/neuroscience-of-gratitude/.

Wisdom Notes

252 **Our autonomic nervous system is made up of:** Porges, *The Polyvagal Theory*, 115–120; Deb Dana, *The Polyvagal Theory in Therapy: Engaging the Rhythm of Regulation* (New York: W. W. Norton & Company, 2018), 29–35.

252 **These neuroceptions are based on three conditions:** Porges, *The Polyvagal Theory*, 19–20, 23–24, 26–27, 115–118.

256 **Instead, the evidence McGilchrist was uncovering:** McGilchrist, *The Master and His Emissary*, 20–25, 169, 300.

259 **There's a lovely story about how mirror neurons:** Iacoboni, *Mirroring People*, 4–6.

261 **In one of many experiments:** Simone Schnall et al., "Social Support and the Perception of Geographical Slant," *Journal of Experimental Social Psychology* 44, no. 5 (2008): 1246–1255, https://doi.org/10.1016/j.jesp.2008 .04.011.

262 **A second piece of research finds Coan:** James A. Coan, Hillary S. Schaefer, and Richard J. Davidson, "Lending a Hand: Social Regulation of the Neural Response to Threat," *Psychological Science* 17, no. 12 (2006): 1032– 1039, https://doi.org/10.1111/j.1467-9280.2006.01832.x.

263 **Exploring how implicit memory can change:** Ecker et al., *Unlocking the Emotional Brain*, 11–15.

264 **The research in memory reconsolidation:** Ecker et al., *Unlocking the Emotional Brain*, 25–30.

265 **In 1988, she published a book, *The Power of Your Other Hand*:** Lucia Capacchione, *The Power of Your Other Hand: A Course in Channeling the Inner Wisdom of the Right Brain* (North Hollywood, CA: Newcastle Publishing, 1988), 15–25.

Jessica Baum's journey to becoming a psychotherapist began in childhood, driven by an insatiable curiosity about the whys of life: why things happen and why emotions feel the way they do. This deep desire to understand the inner workings of the mind and emotions inspired her to pursue a career in mental health counseling, specializing in trauma, attachment theory, and interpersonal neurobiology. Jessica's own personal core belief is centered around the importance of connection. Connection to ourselves, how we relate to others in the world, and how disconnection causes us pain. Using several modalities, she helps individuals and couples find their path back to wholeness.

She has a private group practice, Relationship Institute of Palm Beach, and she is a certified addiction specialist and certified Imago couples therapist with extensive training in EMDR, experiential therapy, and cognitive and dialectical behavior therapies. She helped thousands heal from trauma. She also has a coaching company where she and her team help individuals and couples all around the world. Jessica established herself as a leading voice in understanding and healing attachment wounds with her top-selling book, *Anxiously Attached: Becoming More Secure in Life and Love.* She has been featured in several popular publications and has been covered extensively in national media, on TV, and in top-rated podcasts. To learn more about Jessica, visit jessicabaumlmhc.com.

Also by

JESSICA BAUM, LMHC

01 14